The Art of F&I
Conversations from The Box

By

Lloyd W. Trushel

Lloyd W. Trushel

First Edition: 2020
Printed in the United States of America
ISBN: 978-0-578-62326-9

Praise for The Art of F&I

"THE ART OF F&I - is a great read. It was quick & entertaining with stories told by an F&I guy. His no-nonsense approach to connecting with others is highlighted in this must read. Highlight, underline, and take notes in it. It will be a great addition to your F&I library of knowledge."
Justin Gasman - McCaddon Cadillac Buick GMC, Boulder, CO

"Your book is AWESOME. Hits the nail right on the head with the ART of F&I... [B]est is not about lowest payment but about how you handled the customer and gave them YOUR BEST! Thanks for the book - greatly appreciated and will become a part of my training with F&I Managers."
Dina Gilbert Wilson – Timbrook Kia, Cumberland, MD

"It truly was a great read. So many people can benefit from the wisdom shared. It's put together in an easy to relate to format. Definitely not like many of the other books out there. Simple suggestions to becoming the best F&I Manager FOR YOUR CUSTOMER!! You hit it out if the park, Lloyd!!"
Joe Opolski – Roy O'Brien Ford, St Clair Shores, MI

"Just finished reading The Art of F&I, what a great read. I loved that it confirmed to me that I'm doing the right things in the box and having story time with customers to earn their trust and presenting protections in a way the helps them. I'm glad I picked this book up."
Alex Clark - Garber Chrysler Dodge Jeep Ram, Saginaw, MI

"Thank you for writing this book. Your book spoke to my heart. I love helping people, I have a heart for service! Your explanation about how our brains work explained a lot about me, to me! Also- your personal note that was in your book was very thoughtful. Nice touch!"
Renee Schmidt Birman - Cloquet Ford Chrysler, Cloquet, MN

"Great book! Easy read. Everyone in the dealership should read it."
Michele Ryan – Royal Subaru, Cortland, NY

"F&I Manager or not, this book is a fantastic read. Overall, the tools in this book will help create a unique experience for the people you engage with. So many great points on trust, being genuine and balancing the customer's needs with your own. Would love to chat with anybody that has read it and wants to share some good vibes."
Tim Buich – ForeverStart

"Things are not the same as they were 20 years ago, but F&I training has not changed. This is the best approach to being an F&I manager. When we realize it's about the customer and the customer experience, we will organically sell more products. I have been in the industry for 20 years and I can tell you that this would have changed my world if I had this when I started - if you are in F&I you need the book..."
Joe Romero – Subaru Security Plus, Portland, OR/Denver, CO

"A refreshing take on F&I process, steering away from the classic "objection handling" tone that most F&I training leans toward. This book is truly about providing the "Best Ownership Experience"(TM) for your clients while remaining profitable. Highly recommended to F&I Managers or really to anyone working in the automotive sales industry."
John Grimaldi – Go Nissan North, Edmonton, AB

"I enjoyed the fresh feel for a new approach in the box"
Mary Ann Palmer – Lakeview Ford, Conneaut Lake, PA

"If the customer experience is something you want to improve, then The Art of F&I is your starting point."
Walt Dobrowski – Principal Warranty Company

"I had my best month ever after finishing the book!
Shawn Trice – Don Ayers Honda, Fort Wayne, IN

"The book is great. It's completely changed my view on everything beyond F&I"
Jay Miranda – Herb Chambers Honda, Boston, MA

Dedication

I would like to dedicate this book to Jennifer who stood by my side while I learned the material. It was a difficult journey from *"Great news, the bank included an approval for an extended warranty! Now sign here and press hard"*, to having real, authentic conversations with people about helping them towards what I now refer to as The Best Ownership Experience™.

Her character and ethics have humbled me over the years and helped guide me down the right path. Through her, I have learned that being focused on doing the right thing as opposed to trying to protect my ego, leads to more profitable transactions, and a more emotionally satisfying life.

In short, she is my guiding light, and my best friend.

Thanks Jen.

Table of Contents

⚠ WARNING

If you're reading this book with the expectation of a handbook, a technical guide, or maybe "10 actionable tips to raise your PVR" this may not be the book for you. Instead, this is a journey into the minds of our customers, and the behaviors happening inside our dealerships. It's less about learning closes, and more about developing process. Instead of word-tracks, we'll talk about critical thinking, and true intent.

*"I write this, not for the many, but for you;
Each of us is enough of an audience for
each other"*

- Epicurus

Introduction

There are many books on how to succeed in F&I. Experts are everywhere trying to give you advice on how to be successful. You see magazines, blogs, podcasts, and even TV shows, telling you how to "maximize your profits" and "overcome any objection". Yet, something is still missing.

Customer satisfaction is incredibly low. People dislike the buying process. Nearly 6 out of every 10 customers skip buying a vehicle service contract from their selling dealer, while third party competition is thriving on selling to those same customers.

With the advent of DealerTrack and RouteOne, coupled with the evolution of the desk submitting deals before F&I involvement even begins, people should be delighted with the overall transaction times, but they're not.

Another problem we face is that most F&I training offered today follows an old model of trying to simply overcome objections. The focus on objections made companies like Pat Ryan and Jim Moran a solution for dealers wanting to create their own F&I departments in the 1970's. And it worked. They created an industry.

But the world keeps moving. Today endlessly debating with customers by overcoming every objection is a problem. We must be as Bruce Lee said, "*Like water*", and adapt to each customer individually.

For instance, today a menu presentation with every product bundled into the "Complete" or "Platinum" column may be the best way to present your payments... or it may not be. Do you know what sales process is most effective in YOUR store? Or...are you just doing what the trainer tells you works best? More importantly, can *they* bring data? Can *they* demonstrate effective results in YOUR store?

If not, why are *they* giving you advice?

The truth is; different methods and behaviors work differently in different cultures. In other words, one size does not fit all. Yet, we engage in a one size fits all, "300% rule" environment that has many F&I managers telling the

customer that *"these are mandatory disclosures"* to <u>sell</u> products. Like it's mandatory, enforced by law, or something. Overall, this doesn't work very well, and your customers agree with me. I propose there is a better way.

<u>To be clear, my goal is not to help you sell more products and make more gross. It's about engaging in behaviors that organically create more product sales, and more gross.</u> Because your customer wants to be protected, everyone does. They just don't like the way coverage is being offered...

Lastly, the framework, and many of the concepts of inside this book will reappear because the ideas interweave with each other.

You may wish to adopt some of the principles in this book into your everyday life. Each little piece will not only help you in the box, but also with every other relationship that you hope to find success in.

The stories are about F&I, but the principles are about life.

I sincerely hope you enjoy our time together.

Be well,

Lloyd Trushel
Seattle, Washington
May 2020

P.S. This material was written and compiled over a few days, but it encompasses the observations, experiences, and ponderings, of nearly 30 years in the car business - mostly focused on F&I development.

I welcome your feedback and hope for your dialogue, so please reach out.

F&IQ
TRAINING & DEVELOPMENT

F&IQ Training & Development
www.FandIQ.com

"The moment there is a suspicion about a person's motives, everything he does becomes tainted."

– Gandhi

Chapter 1

Behaviors

Cust #1 was borrowing 147% of book and she said, *"No. I think I'll pass"* on GAP coverage because *"$14 more is too much right now"*, but she had $100 worth of worthless scratch'd-off Lotto tickets in her trade.

Cust #2 said *"If it breaks, I'll just pay for it"*, but right now he has zero money down and is trading a vehicle with zero maintenance records.

Cust #3 Cut me off and said, *"Nope!"* (No reason given)

12

Then pushed the menu back at me.

If you've spent any time in a dealership, you've met these same customers.

Most of us have been in a sales class, where at some point, the trainer begins carrying on about the COST vs. VALUE equation. How, *"when Value exceeds Cost, even by a penny, the customer always buys"*, but that is not true. And even if it were the truth, what happens when the customer never allows you to get that far?

How about the guy that was surfing on his phone the whole time you were trying to tell him, *"All cars eventually breakdown, so you should buy the coverage!"*, but he just tuned you out...

Did his deal get in your head a little bit? Maybe you missed a good deal while he was in your office? Were you thinking "There goes my PVR, or my Bonus?

What is your strategy for dealing with customers that are NOT engaged and NOT interested in listening to your presentations? Do you have one?

Many finance managers operate in the mode of saying *"These are mandatory disclosures"* or *"It's my job"*. But really, does the customer care about your obligation to do sales presentations?

No. Most don't care, and now you begin to *feel* pressure to "sell something". So, you begin thinking about <u>YOUR</u> PVR, <u>YOUR</u> penetration, <u>YOUR</u> profit and <u>YOUR</u> payplan, or maybe just keeping <u>YOUR</u> job.

But this thinking is focused in the wrong direction. This thinking is focused on you, not them, and they can *feel* it. So, they begin making judgments about you and your motives. Some will decide that you're just doing your job, others might decide you're being pushy, or even rude.

They might ask, *"Do I have to decide right now?"*. You'll say *"no"*, then continue to explain why the best time is now, but it's often too late – you've already missed the sale.

Communicating with the customer and making a sale is completely within reach, but often we miss the signals. In the beginning of the transaction, there wasn't a stop light. It was still yellow, but because we have been conditioned to "hurry up", we pushed for a sale. In short, we sped up, when we should have slowed down.

This might be the easiest concept in the world to understand. Everyone gets it, but it is also incredibly hard to do anything about it. Basically, it's hard to focus on your customers in a meaningful way when you are always under pressure to perform.

You are always reminded about your PVR, penetration and profit, by your peers, sales management, your General Manager, the warranty rep, etc... and even on the best month you're going back to zero soon.

Given this situation and those beliefs, we must wonder if it's possible to create quick and easy transactions and still even make a profit.

SOME OBSERVATIONS

As of this writing, I'm approaching 30 years in the automotive business. I began training F&I managers in 1995 and during that period of time, I've never found the perfect close. I've never found anyone that can inspire the customer to purchase products 100% of the time.

That said, I'm going to share with you what I have learned about the most successful finance managers that I've personally worked with - and learned from over the years. Their behaviors were not able to persuade 100% of their customers either, but they consistently had much higher numbers than their peers. Just like a professional athlete, they didn't win every game but throughout their career they still outperformed everyone else.

They added value to everything they did by exuding professionalism. They created a culture of "team" with their co-workers. In some cases, they established harmony where it did not previously exist before.

I remember working with a group of 14 F&I managers back in 2002. Two of the fourteen F&I managers within the group employed these traits. They had the most consistent numbers in the group. They had the highest VSC penetration in the group too – 60-65% on average. In arguably, what is one of the hardest brands to sell VSC's in, Honda.

These guys never fussed about anything. They just came to work and solved problems. Their GM loved them and so did the rest of the dealership – even accounting.

I remember training them on menu presentations and word tracks. In large part, they just pacified me. Yes, they were model students, and would role play on word-tracks, but they didn't "actually" use word-tracks - they didn't have to. Their behaviors leading up to the customer's decision solicited *"yes"* early in the transaction. They didn't need to practice overcoming objections because there weren't very many. If the customer said no, then no problem. Which seems counterintuitive, I'm sure, but many said "yes" early and often. Those that were on the fence would usually buy with just a little bit more data. Yes, data, not scare tactics or hard closes.

Their approach was more like speaking with a good doctor or lawyer. Sharing valuable information and opinions with the goal of allowing the patient, or client, to make an informed/intelligent decision. No extra "push" was needed, just clear intelligent communication.

The "push" is something that we create within ourselves out of our need to chase our goals. This is great in many areas of life, but too much can cause challenges in the box. If your customer begins to *feel* the "push", they will begin pushing too, and this is where we often lose them. This is when we hear customers say *"Nope!", "Can I think about it?" and "Do I have to decide today?".*

17

Therefore, if we want to communicate with them, we must get our goals aligned before we interact with our customers. We must know what our agenda is. We must identify what it is that we are actually "pushing" for. Basically, are we trying to help the customer? Or are we just trying to help ourselves?

In Latin, they have a phrase, *"Cui bono"*, which translates to English as *"Who benefits?"* So, be clear and ask yourself Cui Bono?, *"Who benefits if the customer buys your product?"*

If a customer *feels* like a victim because they don't understand something, or they *feel* like you're trying to scare them, they'll "pull" away. If instead, your conversation is about creating the Best Ownership Experience™, then some people that wouldn't normally listen to you will decide to tune in.

Basically, our intent is super-important here because people *feel* it. So, we must get our intent right before we engage with them. If you're trying to do something to them, like sell them product X, it will *feel* pushy. But if your goal is for them to have great experience, it will *feel* completely different.

Creating this difference is what will separate you from being just another salesperson.

METHODOLOGY

How do you take a product that has been in decline since the early 1990's and turn it around during a recession? First, you collect data on your actual customers and then customize your behaviors around them.

In 2009, Subaru tried this approach by marketing primarily to educators, health-care workers, technology professionals, "outdoorsy" types, and single female heads of households. In their wisdom, <u>no one else bought Subaru cars, so no one else really mattered</u>. They hired Martina Navratilova, a lesbian and former tennis pro, as their spokesperson. As a result, some people threatened to boycott the brand, but Subaru didn't buckle under the pressure. Subaru knew the group boycotting them wasn't really in their demographic anyway.

Additionally, Subaru sales were going up while the rest of the car business was falling apart. Remember, in 2009, 1,550 franchise dealers went out of business that year, followed by another 760 in 2010. Yet, Subaru managed to begin a climb that still hasn't stopped.

Like Subaru, you must niche and focus narrowly, until you have a process that communicates the perfect message. This became evident to me in 2009, while the car business was shifting from the recession.

Like Subaru, I began to study consumer behavior habits and focused communication myself. I found connections in dealership behavior that directly affected PVR and Penetration rates. I learned how we could modify our behavior to not only be more profitable, but also the path to enjoying our work a lot more.

I spent a lot of time studying how the brain works. Specifically trying to understand how people make decisions. In the process, I discovered a couple basic laws about F&I.

F&I LAW # 1 – TRUST IS THE MOST VALUABLE CURRENCY IN THE WORLD.

Trust is universal. Regardless of what country you're in or what language you speak - it is more valuable than money.

Trust is quite simply a gateway. Your customer will decide whether you can be trusted before listening to your menu presentation or considering at any data that supports them buying a product from you.

In other words, No Trust = No Sale.

F&I LAW # 2 - IT IS DYSFUNCTIONAL NOT TO WANT THE MOST WARRANTY AVAILABLE ON ANYTHING.

No matter what product you buy you will want guarantees.

Also, you will always want the longest guarantee available. You may not be willing to buy more coverage, but you will always want the most coverage available and the more the better.

Basically, we all want guarantees.

NATURALLY COMPETITIVE PEOPLE

Could the need to "win" play into the decision to skip a VSC or GAP? Is it possible, at least some of your customers, will *feel* this way when you begin your presentation? Absolutely!

Maybe those customers are part of the "group" that always tries to maximize or stretch every cent of value out of every transaction. The desire to do so isn't always as rational as cost vs. value. Sometimes, it's just an emotional response. Emotionally, some people *feel* the need to win in exchanges and transactions.

Would it surprise you if I said there is no such thing as a group that always does that? Would it surprise you that the truth is; independently, people respond to all purchases differently, and there is rarely a code of disciplined behavior that all people keep.

As author, Yuval Noah Harari, explains in his book, <u>Homo Deus – A Brief History of Tomorrow,</u> *"we decide - and then we justify our actions"*. Basically, that we make "gut" decisions and then tell ourselves a story that justifies that decision. An example of this would be a customer that has decided that all salespeople are cheats and liars. This is only a gut decision, but it will be justified by "that one time" something happened. Often, the decision is not based on solid data.

In the box, this can result in your customer declining your products before the presentation even begins. This is a tough place to start, yet it happens all the time.

By understanding some basic consumer behaviors, and maximizing your best behaviors, we can radically reduce the amount of resistance we receive right from the beginning.

If your customer lacks Trust, Need, or Belief, they will never consider the Cost vs. Value equation.

On the other hand, when we establish trust, people will listen, and communicate openly about their needs and beliefs. Then concerns like cost, payments, or anything else that needs to be addressed before they can agree to buy your products can occur.

THE COST VS. VALUE MYTH

For years I've heard sales trainers say, *"When value exceeds cost, the customer will always buy"*, but it's not exactly true. Let's discuss what cost and value actually mean.

Costs are relatively fixed, and we have some control over them. Inventory, advertising, reconditioning, compensation, interest rates, and insurance products are all pretty similar across the car business. It's rare that one dealership has a unique advantage in these areas.

Value, on the other hand, is about belief, it's an opinion. Value doesn't care about cost. Value is determined by how someone *feels* in the moment.

Eventually, you're going to have to answer the customer's question when they ask, *"How much is the VSC or GAP"*, and in that moment the customer is going to begin making judgments. They will begin making assumptions and associations based on your pricing and the way you deliver that information. The value of your products are going to be determined by your customer's opinion.

Value can be heavily influenced by data, and time, but value is still perceived. As a result, value can still sometimes just be an illusion.

Tonight, you can go outside and hold a penny up in front of the moon. You'll see Abraham Lincoln's head is almost as big as the moon, but of course it's not.

It's just an illusion created by distance. If the penny was farther away than your arm's length away, the illusion would disappear. Time influences value the same way.

If we lengthen the amount of time before an F&I product is needed, its perceived value lessens.

If we shorten the time, then the perceived value increases.

It's that simple.

Test it below ⬇

Imagine yourself at the airport rushing to catch a red-eye flight. You're super hungry, so you grab a peanut butter & jelly sandwich from the gift store. The cashier asks you for $6.49 and you think that's kinda pricey for a basic PB&J. Heck, you could buy a loaf of bread, peanut butter, and jelly for about the same cost at a grocery store.

But, with no time left to find other options, the value of the sandwich grows. You buy it now or risk being hungry for the next six hours, and suddenly, (as you can see from my receipt) it's worth it!

```
                        Tampa International Airport
            Thank you for shopping with us! If you
            have any questions or concerns, email
            us at customerservice@newslinkgroup.net
   COKE 20 OZ PK24
   PEANUT BUTTER & JELLY  490440
        1060000003                          2.49 *

                                            6.49 *
   SUBTOTAL
   SALES TAX                               $8.98
   TOTAL                                   $0.63
   VISA                                    $9.61
   ======================================= $9.61
   PURCHASE $9.61
   ************3087 Visa
              CHIP READ
   REF#: 019660 Approved

   Visa Credit
   A0000000031010

   TC - 9743BD54930C5554

   TRUSHEL/LLOYD W
   Mode: Issuer
```

"People don't care how much you know until they know how much you care."

- Theodore Roosevelt

THE IMPOSSIBLE "F" CUSTOMER

In 1995, I learned about the "F" customer in an F&I class that I attended, and they are still a challenge today. I was taught that approximately 10% of all customers are laydowns, 80% must be closed, and the 10% remaining…They were "F" customers.

I commonly heard that statements like: *"These customers do not budge"*, *"They never buy anything from us"* and *"They are impossible"* We've all heard the phrase, *"Misery loves company"* and some people just want to fight when they come to buy their cars.

When we've had enough of anything, we may *feel* the desire to fight back, which kinda makes sense when it's directed at the right target - but sometimes the desire to fight becomes a desire to fight about everything, or with anyone. This can even happen when the confrontation is not in our own best interests, like skipping a VSC or GAP coverage, when it's needed.

I think this is some of what drives "F" customers. A deep frustration with something that may, or may not, be related to your transaction. Regardless, if someone is feeling defensive, they are more likely to "tune out" or simply say "no" to your presentation.

I believe the "F" in "F Customer" should actually stand for fear. They could easily be afraid of you, or salespeople in general. They could be uncomfortable because they bought elsewhere in the past and it wasn't a pleasant experience, or they left feeling ripped off by someone that was just being really nice at the time.

Of course, they could just be in fear of a higher payment, when they should really be afraid of a major repair.
So, they must make the choice... Fight or Flight.

Flight is easy to recognize. They'll say something like...
"Can I think about it?" or *"Do I have to decide today?"*.
Often, stalling the decision isn't about considering their options, it's just simply a verbal form of running away.

Fighting is different. It looks like... *"Nah, I never buy any of that stuff"* or *"Don't waste your time"*. I sometimes hear F&I managers explain to me how "dumb" their customers are for skipping a VSC or GAP. This could be true, but it is more likely that a good portion of those "dumb" customers are actually in "fight-mode" and the Finance Manager is misinterpreting their actions.

In her landmark book, <u>The Ego and the Mechanisms of Self Defence</u>, Anna Freud (daughter of Sigmund) coins the phrase "psychological self-defense". She explains that our minds will play tricks on itself, or even lie to itself, if needed for self-preservation. A common example is <u>denial</u>, but then she unpacks 47 more examples of emotions that all people adopt to protect themselves.

When the mind cannot deal with something, it will often rearrange or edit the truth. At least until it's safe to deal with the situation.

Similar behaviors occur in the box. We've all had a customer $5,000 upside down refusing GAP. Why? Again, it's fear, and reflexively they say *"NO"*.

Their fear of being taken advantage of is greater than their fear of skipping GAP coverage.

Getting through this is NOT impossible, but it will take courage and patience on your part.

There are only 2 rules for communicating with "F" Customers:

Rule # 1: You must share some undeniable information with your customer - in a very gentle way.

What kind of "undeniable information" you ask?

The undeniable fact that they actually want to be covered. They want safety, they want to be protected, or otherwise removed from risk. In short, the customer actually wants the Service Contract coverage. They actually want the benefit that GAP gives.

Rule # 2: You need to demonstrate that you actually care about them, and their outcome.

Remember **F&I Law # 2** - It is dysfunctional not to want the most warranty available on anything. No matter what product you buy, you will always WANT a guarantee.

You will always WANT the longest guarantee also. You may not be willing to buy more coverage, but that doesn't mean you don't WANT it. And your customer WANTS it too.

They want the most coverage available, the more, the better. So, what's wrong with reminding the customer that we all want guarantees? And that they should at least review the product, and then make "an informed decision".

Nothing, as long as you're also obeying rule # 2. Being genuinely concerned about your customer's future.

This allows you to authentically discuss the value of the VSC, GAP or other products with them without triggering their Fight or Flight response.

Test it below

If possible, give an example of a time you volunteered or forfeited your warranty coverage on anything?

You probably can't think of one. Because it would be dysfunctional, even irrational to decline a product guarantee.

In short, we KNOW people want guarantees. We KNOW more warranty is desired as opposed to less.

People may not want to pay for it, but they do want the "guaranteed" feeling. We all do, on every product we buy, every time. Not wanting the longest guarantee on any product would be dysfunctional. It would be irresponsible. Right?

BAD F&I TRAINING

Most of today's F&I training was designed in the 1980's & 1990's. Boom years, robust financial growth, and times were good. But today things are much different. The culture of America is different than it was in the 1990's.

Times have changed. Accordingly, the F&I training from the 80's & 90's has become ineffective and obsolete in many ways. Getting five (5) *"NO"'s* from your customer is a problem. In fact, trying to *"overcome objections"* is a problem.

We need to behave in a manner that does not create objections in the first place.

Almost every time someone outside the auto industry asks me what I do, I receive a response that includes a horror story about buying or not buying a car. Experiences like a an acquaintance who bought a Mazda, and her story about 3 different managers taking TO's trying to close her on a VSC. They failed, but their customer is still telling people the story of how she *"Loves the car, but not the dealer... and she'll never buy from them again"*.

Because of bad F&I training, F&I departments are on the chopping block in some stores. I see examples all over YouTube demonstrating old school training methods.

One video, "Alexa Amenta F&I Presentation", recently pulled down, had nearly 18,000 views. I watched this video and it is exactly the type of training I received in the early 1990's. She graduated in 2016 and was out of the car business a couple of months later.

This is what I believe is wrong with many F&I departments.

It's unrealistic. No one will sit through 20 minutes of *"blah, blah, blah… buy it or else bad things will happen!"* If they do sit through it, it's because they really want the car, but they are just waiting to say "no", again.

We live in a world of 60 second transactions and this antiquated sales method is dead. In the process of dying, it's also killing our CSI and our profits. I believe it's time for every dealer to abandon the model and embrace the inevitable change.

I'm going to emphasize that there are some amazing trainers out there that grab your attention and they get results. I'm not talking about those guys. I'm talking about the trainer that is only reading word tracks out of a book and role playing scenarios that don't model real-life transactions.

WORD-TRACKS WON'T SAVE YOU

Customers give us objections all the time. We are trained to say the same responses when we hear those objections. This is the nature of word-tracks. It's basically just a pattern of conversation that the customer, although unaware, is supposed to follow.

Entertain for a moment that you're trying to explain why somebody needs gap insurance. *"Mr. customer, blah blah blah blah blah..."* We do it so many times that we develop a pattern.

Let's say that you want to describe a problem. You're going to have a very specific pattern of unpacking that idea for the customer. Similar to a martial artist using a physical pattern to slip or block an attack from their opponent, we use a verbal pattern to describe how someone can benefit from GAP coverage.

Understanding that we are using a pattern, the question then becomes; can we measure, or modify, the effectiveness of our communication patterns?

If we're able to broaden the verbal patterns that we operate within, then we can communicate more effectively with other people. Learning more verbal patterns allows you to be more effective in the conversation. Like having two or three word-tracks for GAP instead of one. You can deploy the word-track you hope will be most effective.

These verbal patterns can be effective, until you meet someone that recognizes the pattern for what it is, a manipulation. Once they see through it, you're in trouble.

A black belt in martial arts is someone who can see and run a lot of different patterns. They are not stuck with two or three. They understand the mechanics and are able to adapt in the moment.

A black belt in F&I doesn't need to follow a script. They possess the ability to go anywhere in the conversation with their customer. They are able to openly discuss products and benefits without fear of where the conversation goes.

This comes from having two very important characteristics; First, is developing a deep understanding of how your products work, how claims are handled, and how the product helps create The Best Ownership Experience™ for your customer. In short, professional competency.

The second is having good intent. If our intent is about doing something "to" the customer, rather than something "for" the customer, we cannot fully be open in our conversations. This comes from hiding the truth or facts from people. If our intentions have a spirit of nobility, then we can open up more fully with the person across from us, we can communicate better and shorten the transaction time. In short, the second component is just having good character.

Our goal, from the very first moment, should be to make sure the customer understands who we are.

In order to do that, we must ask ourselves:

Who I am, do I always operate with integrity and honesty?

Do I know how to perform my job at the highest professional level?

Because, if I'm only there for the money, it's likely I'm not going to put in the work to create the Best Ownership Experience™ for my customer.

And once they discover you're only there for yourself, the transaction will slow down, and the profit will shrink as you try to negotiate through their reluctance. This is where word-tracks fall apart.

"Real combat is spontaneous, not rehearsed"

- Bruce Lee

MEET THE SALES PREVENTION MANAGER

I can't count how many times I have heard people say *"I keep pushing until I get 5 no's!"*. Or sometimes it's *"I don't hear the word no"*. They brag about *"Hammering people"* and *"Ripping heads off"* when they close a big deal, as if the customer didn't see any value in the products offered and it was only their amazing ability as a closer.

Just pounding people with word-tracks is a lack of intelligent focus on the overall F&I process. Too often, the only emphasis is on the immediate profit, and zero thought is given to the future relationship between the customer and the dealership. For some F&I managers, they'll just find another job if they stop making money or their chargebacks become too high.

New F&I managers have a different problem. They receive questionable to sometimes terrible training. Often, the new F&I manager finds themselves in the box without the ability to have a "real world" conversation about the transaction or the products themselves. He/she is only focused on one thing - overcoming objections, which ironically creates more objections.

But, in fairness to everyone I've just mentioned, if they're not making enough profit, they're going to get fired, so they *feel* like they really don't have any choice. As a result, thousands of times a day this type of transaction occurs in dealerships across the country:

39

1st attempt – The Transition
F&I: *"Of all the packages I've shown you, which one makes the most sense for you?"*
CUST: *"None of them"*
F&I: *"It's hard to justify the cost if you can't see the value. May I ask you _____ "* (or similar statement designed to keep asking questions)

2nd attempt – You Told Me (Use the interview against them)
F&I: *"You told me ____ ."*
CUST: *"OK"* (Customer surrenders but is planning to cancel and feels shame about the experience)
OR THEY SAY: *"I SAID NO"* (Customer fights. Also never visits again and leaves negative reviews)

3rd attempt – Scare Tactic (All cars break)
F&I: *"Imagine ___ happens. How are you going to pay the bill?"*
CUST: *"OK"* (Customer surrenders but is planning to cancel and feels shame about the experience)
OR THEY SAY: *"I SAID NO"* (Customer fights. Also never visits again and leaves negative reviews)

4th attempt – The Surprise – (Longer term)
F&I: *"What if I could provide all the benefits of the _____ package and keep your payment the same?"*
CUST: *"OK"* (before chargebacks)
OR THEY SAY: *"No thanks, I don't want a longer term"*

5th attempt - The Discount (Loss of profit and credibility)
F&I: *"What if I could include the _____ package and keep your term and payment the same"?*
CUST: *"OK"* (before chargebacks)
OR THEY SAY: *"I'm really ok with just the car. How much longer is this going to take?"*

These techniques are actually what most people complain about. Many F&I product providers know it's happening, and they overlook it because they don't actually have a quality training solution.

Yes, they have many years of experience, but their experience and training are equally as old. Unfortunately, no one talks about it and many Dealers and GM's are completely unaware.

*"Intelligence
is the ability
to adapt to change"*

- Stephen Hawking

LOW COMMITMENT TO TRAINING?

In a recent poll of F&I managers, 61% felt like their trainer was *"Completely out of touch and hadn't spun a deal in years, if ever"*. Another 23% received zero F&I training at all.

In short 84% of those surveyed felt they were not getting the training support they needed.

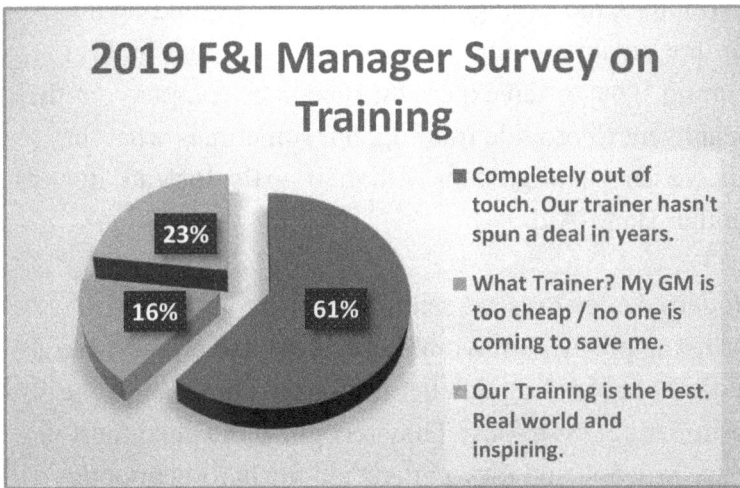

Why does this happen? Most dealers and GM's are simply too busy to assist. They're so focused on advertising, hitting their units, managing costs and keeping (or finding) employees, that F&I development is something they plan on doing later. So, they look for a "plug and play" person that can be up and running quickly. The obvious problem is that the person they found is usually unemployed already – sometimes for good reason.

Of course, this should raise questions like "What happened at their last store that caused them to be unemployed in the first place?"

This perpetual rotation of finding a Band-Aid for F&I may work a little longer, but the F&I experience is often the deciding factor on whether many customers even return to the dealership, so dealers should take note.

As of 2019, the average new car dealer is spending $640 per unit on advertising, but less than $10 a unit on F&I training. They often expect the insurance company, or their local agent to provide training, but sometimes what they receive isn't in alignment with their goals. Instead, it's just another Band-Aid.

Modern dealerships are searching for a solution to shrinking profits, unfavorable reviews, and are desperately in need of providing quicker transaction times once the customer agrees to buy. They recognize the need for a better process, and they understand the hard-economic consequences of what happens when they fail to deliver a quality experience to their customers.

This is just another reminder that endlessly attempting word-tracks, hoping to "overcome objections", does not create lifetime customers. If we are truly building a legacy, we must learn to adopt the behaviors that help customers engage in the process of selecting products with us.

HIGH LEVEL PROBLEM SOLVING

Life is just a series of events. Many of these events are problems. But, sometimes we can "pick our problems".

A small problem, like finding an extra $30 over the next 30 days is pretty manageable for most people.

A bigger problem, like having to pay thousands of dollars to fix your car or payoff a loan this afternoon, is much less manageable.

The truth is that the solution for one problem is the typically the beginning of the next.

Like a customer that skips a VSC, then acquires $2,200 in credit card debt at 18%, just to pay for a repair that they were overcharged by $400 on.

This is a pretty bad day for them, and it could have been easily handed for only $30 a month, but they didn't pick the $30 a month problem.

Occasionally, we can pick our problems. In fact, I would argue that this is our job. To help our customers "pick better problems". An extra $50 a month might be a strain on the budget for some of your customers, but major repairs, gaps in insurance settlements and excessive depreciation from loss of appearance, are much worse.

Just like in life, we have choices. I can pick the problem of eating healthy - less tasty - foods today or experience the problem of poor health tomorrow.

I can pick the problem of finding time to exercise today or have the problem of my body failing tomorrow.

I can pick the problem of reading books to stimulate and educate my mind today or suffer lack of knowledge and understanding tomorrow.

For our customers, they can pick the problem of $35 a month now for the VSC or an $1800 emergency later when they must repair the most important tool they own.

They can pick the problem of $14 a month for GAP, or risk having to pay $3,000 to payoff their car before they can replace it.

The goal here is to solve your customers' problems before they occur. Being good at problem solving leads directly to success, not just in the box, but in most endeavors throughout all of our lives.

Test it below

Take a professional fighter for instance. He or she has a game plan when the fight begins, but if the other fighter is getting the best of them, they must adapt or else they'll lose.

This is problem solving on a very high level. They either make adjustments, and solve problems, or they lose. Period.

The paradox is that the stress goes up fast when it is tied directly to your paycheck. The same thing happens in the box. You've got seconds to figure out how to solve problems or your paycheck is going to be affected.

And just like a fighter, we must train. In our case, "training" is learning how our products help protect our customers. Once you've mastered that, you can go anywhere in the conversation, that the customer takes you. You can make the necessary adjustments and help them choose from the protection packages that solve their problems.

CONFESSIONS OF AN F&I TRAINER

I couldn't do it anymore. The lie. The status quo. Like a teacher telling the happy story of Christopher Columbus to elementary school kids while knowing that the truth is very different.

There I was, sitting in the training room with a new F&I manager. We're about to go through the motions again, presentation, handle objections, print. That is it. That is all he needs to know right now. The idea is simple. Make someone new to the F&I department profitable to the store, immediately.

At least this guy had a foundation as a BDC guy in a prior dealership, and he knew his way around the DMS. He and I had already completed 1 day of basics/laws. On day two, we were 3 hours into the menu presentations session. We broke for lunch to grab tacos in the break room. Then it began…

A conversation. Philosophy, economics, and purpose with the newbie F&I guy. As we go, I recognize he's wicked smart and has some great observations on life as well. I learned a bit.

Later, in class, we're role playing word-tracks. You know, the "all cars break/overall cost of only one repair/99.9%" style stuff. He looks me dead in the eye and seriously asks *"Does any of this shit actually work on people?"*.

My ego speaks, *"Absolutely!"* I announce, without hesitation. We continue training.

I can feel mild cynicism, but we carry on. His mind opens a little to the training and we spend three more days practicing menu presentations and overcoming objections. I leave, and soon his numbers are in the top percentage of my group. Success, right?

Not really, I was still bothered by the question weeks later. I told my wife about this. She told me something profound. Something my ego also couldn't handle. I wasn't practicing what I preach, and I didn't even know I was doing it.

She told me, *"You didn't use word tracks or closes with customers. Most of your transactions were just open conversations with people"*. I'm floored! I can't believe it. But then it occurred to me, the difference between a "close" and an "explanation" can be subtle. I had ways of unpacking information and explaining things, that didn't end with *"would you like your payment to begin in 30 or 45 days?"*.

I didn't overcome objections, I just helped people understand their decisions better. I was communicating gently, and people were moving forward with me, but I was teaching something entirely different. Today, I clearly understand that it wasn't my closes that generated higher profits, it was my care.

"It's hard to get someone to do the right thing, when their paycheck depends on them doing the wrong thing"

- Upton Sinclair

Chapter 2

Communication

Tuesday morning 11:11 A.M. (She's here to cancel)

"Are you who I see to cancel my GAP?" she asked me. I said, *"I'd be happy to help you",* and I pulled up her deal. It's only been three days and she's already refinanced with her credit union - and she bought their GAP!

She tells me they were ½ a point lower and that this will save her $11.00 a month... Then a story about how every little bit counts. I think to ask her *"Does their GAP cover 150% of book, and her deductible up to $1,000?"*, but she doesn't know what it covers, and worse, she has become a little embarrassed at not knowing what she actually bought.

This one question causes her mood to change, and suddenly she's in a hurry to leave.

Now, I know why this situation is falling apart. Her feelings got a little hurt by the embarrassment of not knowing if she made the right decision. For a second, she *felt* a small level of shame in her gut about trusting the credit union.

But then, to *feel* better, she internally told herself the warm-fuzzy story that, its "ok", and... how the credit union people are the good guys and I'm the bad guy. Then she left, not knowing if she only has 120% or 150% GAP coverage, and most likely with the new responsibility of paying a $500 deductible if she has a claim.

In my world, I asked her a legitimate question, about specific coverage, on a legal contract. In her world, she *felt* offended. She framed me as a jerk. Perception is reality, I guess. Still, I suspect I could have possibly saved the products, financing, and CSI, had I connected with her differently.

THE TRUST ALARM

He screamed *"Let's get out of here now!"*. Quickly, all the firefighters followed the chief outside. Moments later the floor collapsed. They all would have died if they had stayed inside.

Afterwards, a reporter asked the chief how he knew to run. *"I didn't even know that I said anything"* the chief responded. It was all subconscious.

Sometimes, this is what people will refer to as a sixth sense. Also known as knowledge that you did <u>not</u> receive from sight, smell, touch, sound or taste. This is information that comes from somewhere else – we regularly refer to this as a "gut" feeling.

So, where does the "gut" feeling come from? In the chief's case it came by way of little things, like his ears burning from an abnormal amount of heat, and from the fire being *"too quiet"*. In the moment, he was not consciously aware of his ears burning or the odd quietness, but he could recall these details after the fact.

His crew thought they were trying to put out a small kitchen fire, but their water didn't seem to have the usual effect. It turns out the actual fire was underneath them, in the basement.

Even though the chief didn't consciously know the fire was in the basement at the time, his gut instinct, based on data and prior life experience, told his subconscious to run. So, he made the call to leave the house.

In the box, you will meet customers that also have a sixth sense. If they *feel* a situation is unsafe, like dealing with someone that is only focused on making money, they're going to run. If you're sending the message that you're only there for you and you're only thinking about your PVR, you're going to have a tough time if their "gut" tells them not to buy or to be careful. At a minimum, the customer is going to withhold their trust from you. <u>Once you lose trust, you are not likely to sell them anything.</u>

Now, we can call it the "Trust Alarm," "Our Sixth Sense" or just plain old "Anxiety". Some customers just come in with their defenses up, right? So, we spend a lot of time training on learning how to close. We dig deep into the sales training handbook in order to overcome their objections. Customers do something similar. They often create strategies for saying *"No"*.

Picture a husband and wife simply out "kicking tires", with a commitment between each other that no matter what, they WILL NOT BUY TODAY. They plot out a story beforehand about refinancing their house, or some other bogus reason, with the intention of lying to the salesperson as to why they can't buy today. Why would they do that?

They're not alone. Consider a telemarketer. Have you ever said you didn't have time, even though you did? Why would a customer plot to lie beforehand? Is it possible they're afraid of us?

In a recent Gallup poll on ethics, we find that "car people" are at the bottom of the list, below lawyers and members of congress. So maybe they are afraid of us.

Please tell me how you would rate the honesty and ethical standards of people in these different fields -- very high, high, average, low or very low?	Very high	High	Average	Low	Very low	No opinion
	%	%	%	%	%	%
Nurses	31	54	14	*	1	*
Engineers	17	49	31	2	1	1
Medical doctors	20	45	28	4	2	*
Pharmacists	15	49	28	5	3	*
Dentists	13	48	33	4	2	*
Police officers	17	37	31	9	5	*
College teachers	12	37	34	10	7	1
Psychiatrists	10	33	43	10	2	2
Chiropractors	6	35	47	9	2	1
Clergy	10	30	42	10	5	4
Journalists	5	23	34	20	17	1
Bankers	3	25	52	15	5	*
Labor union leaders	4	20	48	20	7	1
Lawyers	4	18	49	19	9	*
Business executives	2	18	50	22	8	1
State governors	4	16	52	21	6	*
Stockbrokers	2	12	55	22	8	2
Advertising practitioners	2	11	44	30	10	2
Insurance salespeople	2	11	52	26	9	*
Senators	2	11	42	32	13	1
Members of Congress	3	9	33	34	21	1
Car salespeople	1	8	47	30	13	*

Dec 2-15, 2019
Gallup

https://news.gallup.com/poll/1654/honesty-ethics-professions.aspx

It seems that years of dysfunctional sales practices have led to dysfunctional buying practices. This begs the question; *does customer's anxiety play a major part in the sales process?*

Absolutely! When people are nervous, they don't focus well. They sometimes won't even comprehend or understand your products, or your presentations.

BEING TRUSTWORTHY

We live in a world full of locks. Your door is locked, your car is locked, your computer is locked, your phone is locked, *"Don't forget to lock up when you leave"*, and the list goes on... We are conditioned not to trust, but we still wish we could.

Thousands of years ago, we had to band together to survive. The world was a pretty wild place and we were on the menu for all kinds of predators. We survived through teamwork, *"You sleep and I'll watch out for threats"*. My ancestors and yours needed to cooperate with each other by protecting food, sharing resources and guarding against predators. They had to trust each other, or they would die.

And they did trust each other. Otherwise, you and I wouldn't be here today. Basically, 100% of our ancestors lived long enough to mate and reproduce because of one thing, trust.

Without Trust, mankind simply wouldn't exist.

So, how do we develop trust with our clients and co-workers, as well as, friends and family?

We must walk the walk. We must behave with the qualities of self-trust. When we trust ourselves, people around us see it and *feel* it. It's that simple.

THE POSSIBILITY OF POSSIBILITY

Choice is linked to risk, and risk provokes anxiety. So, being in the situation of having to decide on something like a Vehicle Service Contract "right now" can create varying levels of anxiety for people.

Anxiety is actually a "survival tool". Emphasis on the word "Tool". It's a resource, not something to fear. It's valuable for making sure that you make smart business decisions – like when you're buying a car. It's responsible for the "gut" feeling you get warning you to "slow down" or to "proceed with caution". When you come to realize its functional use as a tool and nothing more, then you understand the value of it.

Anxiety lives in one little part of the brain, called the Amygdala. Its primary job is to decide what is and isn't safe. If something seems unsafe, it begins the "FIGHT or FLIGHT" process. Once that happens, people will begin to tune out, begin delaying on decisions or worse… Perhaps, argue with and then frame you as a pushy jerk.

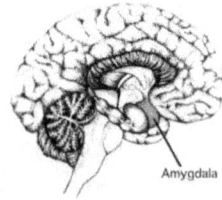

Fortunately, getting past the customer's anxiety is within your power. By establishing trust, you will be able to communicate through your customer's anxiety, which is super important if you hope to discuss the value of your products.

"Anxiety is the price we pay for the human ability to choose"

- Soren Kierkegaard

BUILDING TRUST

Have you ever seen the Tonight Show with Johnny Carson, Jay Leno or Jimmy Fallon? Are you familiar with the opening monologue? You know, the part where he speaks to the audience about current events and makes jokes. Notice, it's not a conversation. He is speaking to them, but they rarely ever speak back.

This is a monologue. In Latin, *Mono* stands for one. One person is talking here, which is perfect for comedy, but not so hot for sales transactions.

We need to establish a dialogue, or more specifically, a two-way conversation, if we hope to effectively communicate ideas, and feelings, with our customers.

In Latin, the word *dia* means to penetrate through. For us, we need to penetrate through all the preconceived ideas our customers arrived with and show them we are not what they expected. It's the only way we can prove we are not just another salesperson.

For this to happen, we will be working with our customers in two different areas:

- The Thinking Self (Logic & Competency)
- The Feeling Self (Character & Ethics)

On the Thinking Self:

It is our ability to create a feeling of safety for our customers, in a way that allows them to freely speak about their concerns. It is our professionalism. It is our knowledge base. It is where logic, and problem-solving live. It is our technique, and our competency.

Our problem-solving skills are necessary if we hope to create the Best Ownership Experience™ for our customers. In our case it means that not only understanding our lenders, laws, and products, but also having the ability to apply critical thought to your customer's needs, then discussing the right product mix that creates the Best Ownership Experience™ for them.

You can be the most well-intentioned person in the world, an honest person, in every way, but if you cannot demonstrate, with competency, how a product helps - you will not be successful.

So, if we're going to be effective, and help our customers achieve the Best Ownership Experience™, we need the ability to communicate in a way that helps people quickly recognize our level of professionalism and competency.

On the Feeling Self:

This is what we often refer to as a "gut" feeling. It is the desire to be fair. It's our ability to *feel* empathy for others. It is where love, art, and passion originate. It is doing the right thing. It is our intent, our purpose, our character.

A good deal of the material F&I managers learn during F&I training are designed for the Thinking Self. Techniques like word-tracks and closes are about making people think, but if those techniques do not serve your intent, your purpose, your character, then everything you do will seem inauthentic or "salesy". It will merely be manipulation.

If our Feeling Self fails to connect, then our customers won't open up and communicate with us, transparency will diminish, and it's highly unlikely that they will ever *feel* safe enough to trust us.

They will believe there are zero reasons to buy what you're trying to sell them. Even when the benefits of the product are clear, the customer will still say *"No"*.

On the other hand, if we can connect, and our customers are comfortable, open and honest with us, we will have a chance.

On putting the Thinking Self and Feeling Self together:

So, let's say we connect. Your Feeling Self has formed an opinion that I'm a pretty good person, yet I fail to bring more intellectual rigor to justify why you could benefit from a product I'm offering. Then, you'll still say *"no"*.

So, when taking the time to build or construct your dialogue with the customers, we must work on both dimensions, Thinking & Feeling, if we hope to inspire trust.

The first dimension is using our Feeling Self by being transparent in our communication and showing that our true intent is to offer and discuss products that truly help. This is grounded in our belief in those products, and our ability to highly endorse those products.

The second dimension is using our Thinking Self by showing our competency, our knowledge, as it relates to our products. Knowing and showing exactly how the proposed product helps people.

<u>To be more concise, we must be knowledgeable, and show our good intent if we hope to generate trust.</u>

Our product knowledge and closing skills are worthless if we can't get past the customer's "GUT FEELING" – the feeling that is causing them to stall in the first place. And our good intentions are worthless if we don't understand how our products actually solve their problems.

CAN YOU BE TRUSTED?

When you display both your Thinking & Feeling self, people will let their guard down and let you in. This is the beginning of trust.

There is a dynamic at play here, between our head and our gut. Our brain recognizes competency, understands data and makes data judgments based on what can be seen. However, our gut makes decisions on what can be *felt*.

So, while I may understand the VSC coverage will only add $7.00 per month to my payment, my gut is telling me something is off – it *feels* too cheap. So, I ask, *"how much does it cost?"* F&I answers, *"It's only $7.00 per month"*. Still zero hard data given. I want to know the cost, but instead we are creating a bottleneck in the flow of communication and reducing trust in our transaction.

The head and gut, or "Thinking & Feeling selves", work together to make decisions, but it's usually the gut or The Feeling Self that wins, and then The Thinking Self goes on to construct a new story to justify the decision that the The Feeling Self has just made.

We see this in relationships. The heart wants what the heart wants. The head knows that likelihood for success isn't ideal, but we can't help being with the person we want anyway because it's what we want – yet we don't even know why.

The same thing happens in transactions. We make decisions with our gut about trust, and then move forward – sometimes even when our heads point out obvious roadblocks.

Sometimes we even tell ourselves the story that "He or she means well, they were just mistaken", because we are so invested in the way something *felt*.

In the box, we must find congruence with our beliefs. We must be real and authentic. In order to inspire belief, we must believe in the products we offer and understand exactly how they will help. If we don't, people will *feel* it in their gut and say "no". They will *feel* like we cannot be trusted, and they will be right.

In short, character comes from your gut. It is the belief that someone will "do the right thing". Competency, on the other hand, comes from our head, and it is the belief that someone "knows what they are doing". Without this combination, you will find difficulty creating long-term success.

COMPETENCY

Knowledge is knowing how to do things correctly. It's technical. Do you know your stuff or are you winging it? Ask yourself, have you ever actually read the fine print of the contracts you sell to people? Do you understand how they work? How hard is it to file a claim? In short, are you an expert on your products and your job? I hope so.

We display our competency by understanding how we can help our customers have the Best Ownership Experience™. Also, by understanding how we can help people avoid economic/financial hardships.

This requires that you slow down and ask questions when you don't fully understand something. Maybe you pick up the phone and call the product provider and see how the claims process works. Maybe even speak with your service advisors. The key point is to learn everything about what you sell, how it works, and how it helps.

When people meet you, they immediately begin making judgments about *"Who you are?"* and *"Can I trust this person?"*. Having confidence helps a lot. Most people develop confidence from experience. If you skip this part, you cannot be an expert. But there's a big plus side to digging in and fully understanding your products. Competency is the cornerstone of confidence and confidence inspires trust.

CHARACTER

Recognizing right from wrong, then choosing right is the foundation of character. Everyone's moral compass is different, but having good intent is still the same. Like the golden rule says: *Do unto others as you would have them do unto you.* (Matthew 7:12)

Basically, treat people like you'd like to be treated. This does not mean losing profits. All businesses have revenue goals, and must create profit to exist, but you don't need to lie or deceive to create it.

Display your character by being fair. By also thinking about your customer's agenda too. Ask yourself *"is this offer fair"*? Would I buy at these terms or would I advise a friend or family member to buy under these conditions?

Again, we must be profitable, and I want to be crystal clear. Businesses have revenue goals and you will have personal revenue goals. Go after them – just don't lose your ethics or self-esteem in the process.

Anytime a customer asks you, "How much is it?", you should be able to look them directly in the eye and answer. But if you *feel* the urge to hide the truth, it is a sign that you're not feeling comfortable. As a result, your body language, vocal tone and eye movement will begin to betray you.

"When we are being inauthentic our nonverbal and verbal behaviors begin to misalign. Our facial expressions don't match the words we're saying. Our postures are out of sync with our voices. They no longer move in harmony with each other; they disintegrate into cacophony"

– Amy Cuddy

IS IT IN OUR DNA TO LIE?

Koko was
a gorilla
(image)
that was
born in
captivity
and she
learned
how to
interact
with
humans
through
sign language.

As an adult, she was given a kitten. One day, while angry, Koko ripped the sink out of the wall and then blamed it on the kitten. We can assume she saw lying as her only defense when the researchers asked her what happened.

A lie is basically a psychological self-defense. We all have done it. We are just trying to use our intellectual tools to protect ourselves. But we never *feel* good about lying, do we? No. People that lie and *feel* good about it are called psychopaths. Most of us empathize simply because we have experienced the feeling of being lied to - and we didn't enjoy it.

71

YELLOW LIGHTS

Imagine if we connected with people before we discussed products. Is it at least a possibility, our conversations could go differently? Maybe not all the time, but at least a certain percentage of the time.

One way of seeing this is by asking yourself, *"How can I become more than just another salesperson in their eyes?"*

Everyone you meet is fighting a battle you know nothing about.

Be kind.

Always.

Is it possible that you could slow down, be completely authentic, and become the most positive part of their day?

Could you possibly get a real smile from them? Could you maybe add so much value that they leave with respect for your knowledge and professionalism?

This will not occur if you're in a hurry.

This may seem counter-intuitive, but it's "OK" to slow down when you see the yellow lights.

Yes, I know the next customer is waiting and the sales manager is staring at you through the window. I know it's added pressure, but let's consider the transaction from a couple different angles.

From the perspective of the dealership itself: like any business, profit is its lifeblood. So, making a profit and keeping it is super important. The better transaction we have with the customer, and the better chance they have of understanding the value of our products. This leads to more sales and lower chargebacks.

From the perspective of the customer: it is at least a possibility that they might want to have a nice experience with you? Is it possible that they might want something to "go right" in their lives, and it's supposed be this car?

With that in mind, ask yourself, *"How can I use my communication skills to improve their day, my day and meet my dealership's goals?"* Answer that question and you'll immediately become a better F&I manager.

Stop worrying about transaction times. If you're a profitable team-player, you'll earn the freedom to discuss changes that will speed up the transaction process. I can prove it.

Increase your PVR and see how quickly your GM and Sales managers forgive the extra few minutes…

But, soon there won't be any extra time to worry about. Because when we inspire trust, people say "yes" earlier in the transaction.

Let's address the "hurry" everyone seems to be feeling. The interesting thing that everyone seems to be missing is two-fold:

1. The reason the customer is in a hurry is because they are no longer enjoying the process. Make it enjoyable and that hurry begins to evaporate. As they say, *"Time flies when you're having fun"*.

2. The reason the transaction is taking too long is because of the lack of trust. If you silence the "Trust Alarm" the process will speed up. If you set off the "Trust Alarm" the process will slow down.

If the customer doesn't trust you, or your product, and fears being ripped off, everything will go slowly.

If the salesperson on deck doesn't trust you'll spin the current deal quick enough and his customer will change their mind, it will seem too long.

If the sales manager took a short deal and doesn't trust your ability to make it up on the back, he will fear having to explain why he took such a short deal.

Basically, when we have an overall lack of trust it always creates fear.

Ever have someone read the fine print on every form? This is an extreme lack of trust. This is a yellow light, so slow down and address it.

Be authentic and ask them if they had a bad experience in the past, then promise to be completely honest and offer to slow down even more. Change their perception of car people, by showing that you care.

Bring your character and competency, your knowledge and integrity, your head and gut, your Thinking and Feeling self to the customer, and the process will quicken.

PERCEPTION IS REALITY

88% of Americans believe they have superior driving skills compared to most. Obviously, this cannot be true.

People in general, *feel* that their skill level is above average in leadership skills, personal health and ethics - just to name a few.
In a strange twist, the less qualified people are, the most confident they tend to be.

WE SEE
WHAT
WE
WANT

This is referred to as the Dunning-Kruger Effect. Discovered in 1999, it hypothesized that people are confused in two ways. First, they often fail at skills. Second, they lack the understanding to clearly understand the cause of their failure.

Once people slow down and educate themselves, they are quick to admit their mistakes. But most don't take the time to educate.

On the other hand, smart people make the mistake of thinking everyone else is smart enough to understand them. This too has the same effect of creating an inaccurate self image. Too dumb, you can't understand how you're wrong. Too smart, you can't understand that other people don't understand you.

These are all beliefs, which are a strange thing. If we don't believe anything bad will ever happen to us, it's going to be hard to convince us to prepare for it. If I don't believe I'll ever use your product, I'll have a hard time buying it.

In order to inspire change you must believe in change.

Belief is a two-way street. Nobody is going to believe in you if you don't believe in yourself. A lack in your self-confidence it is something that other people will *feel*. If you're lacking confidence, people will notice.

What determines our level of self-esteem is in direct relationship with our habits, and our principals. Having the discipline of acting a certain way to achieve your goals, builds it up. Ignoring the work of living by your principals, destroys it.

You must live in accordance with your beliefs if you wish to be credible. In the box, this means you must also see value in the same products you sell.

TYPES OF TRUTH

When we are trying to create trust, it is assumed we must discuss the truth. I mean, how else can someone trust you if you're not telling the truth. But what is the truth?

Is it always the truth that someone needs the product you're offering? Probably not, but you have economic goals, so you probably ask for the sale even when you're not sure if they need it. But how do you know? Even the smartest person in the world cannot predict with certainty what the future holds.

Ultimately, there are two different types of truth:

- Absolute Truth
- Believed Truth

An example of absolute truth is gravity. Gravity doesn't care if you believe in it. Gravity is always there whether you want it or not.

Money, however, is not absolute. It is believed. We all agree it has value and if our values changed so would its value. Money can feed you, but you cannot eat it. If the belief in money's value changes, it could become worthless. Its utility comes from our mutual belief in its value.

Likewise, with the products we offer. We are never working with absolute truth, only believed truth. Will the car breakdown? Who knows...?

Will having coverage make you *feel* better while you own it? I think we can all agree it will.

CONVERSATION IS NOT COMPREHENSION

We usually don't know much about our customers. We don't know their needs, have much time to explore their driving habits, or their ownership goals. So, we often end up wondering what we can SELL them as opposed to understanding their actual situation. Maybe we subscribe to the 300% rule, offering them everything, hoping that they'll bite on something. In short, we guess. Why?

#1 reason: We fear we will kill the deal by taking too long.

#2 reason: We fear engaging in conversation - We may look uninformed on our products.

#3 reason: We skip trying to understand people, because it's just easier to offer everything.

Unfortunately, the more we guess, the more likely it is that we will be wrong. If our goal is really about helping our customers have The Best Ownership Experience™, then we have the right, and the obligation, not to simply guess.

We often mistake _conversation_ with _comprehension_. We assume that because we understand what something means to us, that it must mean the same to everyone else, too. To avoid guessing, we need to listen carefully to the words and phrases our customers use, and then ask them what those words and phrases mean to them. In other words, clarify.

Here is an example of a pattern I like to use to clarify information with somebody:

Customer: *"I don't want a high interest rate"*

F&I: *"If I asked 10 different people what they considered <u>high</u>; I'd get 10 different answers. May I ask what <u>high</u> means to you?"*

Customer: *"I don't know, probably ___%...", "My bank/credit union offers___%..." or "I didn't want to pay over ___%"*

Sometimes, when we ask the customer to clarify their words, we learn <u>something</u> that we didn't expect, and that <u>something</u> can be even more valuable than we anticipated.

FRAMING YOUR CONVERSATION

Unless you're working for the power company or the DMV, you're not going to sell everyone.

In order to sell more often, you'll need to model your pitch to your audience. For instance, if your customer is very affluent, then a product that provides "budget protection" may not seem very important to them.

However, that same product, discussed from a different point of view, could "save them time" or "create comfort". Now, it may be appealing enough to buy. This is what we refer to as "Framing". Framing helps people see the benefit as it applies to them.

If you're into prestige, I will frame my conversation around your comfort and convenience. If you're very concerned about your budget, then I'll frame the discussion around helping you save money. Ideally, I am going to listen to you, and then frame the conversation around helping you add comfort, avoid pain, or possibly... Both.

Can we simply ask our customer, *"Hey, what's important to you?"* Time, money, something else? Yes, you can, and it will work, if it's genuine. The goal here is to be genuine at trying to help people have the best experience. Doing that opens up the door to these types of communication.

THE SCIENCE OF FRAMING *(PROSPECT THEORY)*

In the box, and in life, we sometimes frame things in a way that keeps us, or our customer, from really understanding a problem. Could the way that we present a product influence how much risk a person will choose to take? Yes, it can and if you have been in F&I for more than a month, you've experienced it. One small phrase, framed negatively, in your presentation can quickly translate into a customer saying *"No"* reflexively.

Nobel prize winning economists Daniel Kahneman and Amos Tversky developed a theory about this called Prospect Theory. It describes how people make decisions (like financial decisions) based on how the information *felt*, rather than the actual information itself.

For instance, if we use "risk" as a closing tool, (i.e. mechanical breakdown), we are more likely to see the customer adopt a "risk seeking" mindset.

Instead, if we use "benefit" as a closing tool, the customer is more likely to adopt a "benefit seeking" mindset. Ultimately, a blended approach is often necessary, but I always recommend beginning with the benefits.

According to Kahneman & Tversky, presenting a problem as a potential loss actually adds momentum to "risk seeking behavior" and framing a situation as a gain adds momentum to "risk-aversion behavior"

83

Test it below ⬇

Imagine for a moment that you work in a large dealership with a few hundred other employees. Financially, the store is experiencing some losses and their General Manager has decided that 60 layoffs are necessary.

To assist the General Manager, the Dealer Principal has brought in two outside consulting firms to see if there's any way to save the 60 jobs.

(On the next page, imagine your GM asked for your opinion. Please make note of your choices)

Make note of your choices:

<u>ABC Consulting proposals:</u>

Solution A:
20 jobs will be *saved*.

Solution B:
1/3 probability that all the jobs will be *saved*
and
a 2/3 probability that none of jobs will be *saved*.

Which solution do you favor?
A or B

<u>XYZ Consulting proposals:</u>

Solution C:
40 people will *lose* their jobs.

Solution D:
1/3 probability that nobody will *lose* their jobs
and
a 2/3 probability that everyone will *lose* their jobs.

Which solution do you favor?
C or D

Now that we have your responses, let's examine the typical responses:

We have found on average that people answer the first and second question differently.

The first question is predominantly answered by being risk adverse (solution "A") and the second question is predominantly answered by exhibiting risk-seeking tendencies (solution "D").

So, what's going on? The two situations are basically identical, and the questions are statistically the same, but they consistently elicit different answers.

The only difference is that the first question focuses on the amount of jobs that might be "<u>saved</u>" and the second question focuses on the amount of jobs that might be "<u>lost</u>".

When we frame a situation as a potential gain by using the word "saved", as in solutions A&B, we see people behaving much more risk-averse. When we frame the situation as a potential <u>loss</u>, as in solutions C&D, we see people behaving with more risk-seeking behavior.

<u>The point is that we can see the same person fluctuate from risk-seeking behavior to risk aversion behavior just because we asked the question differently.</u>

We find that the way we frame the situation, by small changes in wording or language, directly influences our propensity to take or reject risks. In other words, the way we define the problem dictates the way our customer responds to it.

So, how does this work in the box?

Ask yourself how often does the "ALL CARS BREAK" close work on a person buying their 4th Honda because they've never had a problem? Not very well, but why?

F&I Managers are traditionally taught to close based on loss or risk, (i.e. mechanical breakdown or economic hardship). According to Prospect Theory, framing the purchase as a potential problem encourages the customer to become more of a risk-taker. So, instead of a sale, you get to hear, *"I'll take my chances"*.

To avoid encouraging "risk-seeking" behavior, we must talk about benefits and solutions first. Then, only if necessary, discuss the possible loss, or risk, you're trying to protect them from experiencing.

GOOD

This is a personal story, but I believe it demonstrates the effectiveness of slowing down for the yellow lights and engaging the "Thinking Self". Then reframing your view.

We lost an important client in January 2018 that represented a sizable percentage of our company's revenue. Immediately, for about 15 minutes after receiving the news, I was stunned – my "Feeling self" was very engaged.

Honestly, I never anticipated it. The relationship was leveraged nicely in their favor. We provided a higher level of service than expected, and the relationship was mutually open and helpful.

But our client hired a new CEO. And just like hiring a new head coach, he had existing relationships with people he already liked and trusted. He gave us "the ax" on his second day without even comparing our companies. I was at a loss - professionally stunned. I had to ask myself, *"Do I frame this new situation as a threat… or an opportunity?"*

Yes, it is a threat to my income and my ego. Both of those make sense. But… where were the hidden opportunities? After calming my "Feeling self", I spent a few minutes with my "Thinking Self". Then, I began to consider this new circumstance from multiple angles, I saw things clearly, and it changed my life in a couple huge ways.

For the last several years, I was spending nearly 150 nights a year, away from home, for this one client. I was traveling endlessly, and I was exhausted.

The extra time allowed me to do what I wanted, and I wanted to spend it with the people closest to me. The connection and conversations that I wanted with my wife and children were difficult to acquire. Everyone was always busy, and I was always working or gone. I wanted to travel to places other than dealerships. (No offense).

So, I reframed my thinking and decided to see the GOOD in the new situation. I bought an RV and we traveled with my daughter, who just graduated from high school, for a whole year.

We had the experience of staying in the Rocky Mountains just outside Denver, on a dude ranch in Cheyenne, floating in the Great Salt Lake, being deep in the forest outside Seattle, in the weirdness of Portland, on a cliff overlooking the Pacific Ocean in San Francisco, in the Redwood Forest outside Santa Cruz, in Hollywood, Las Vegas and Vancouver too. Also, some of the most desolate places in America like Meteor Crater, The Petrified Forest, The Grand Canyon, the Navajo Nation, and Antelope Canyon (image). We spent several weeks in each location. It was great!

None of this would have happened without slowing down my "Feeling self" and allowing my "Thinking self" to work.

Stopping the anxiety and fear of the unknown long enough to embrace the new opportunity of working from the road and spending time seeing the country with my family.

Truly, it was a once-in-a-lifetime trip.

Visiting Antelope Canyon, Arizona, with my daughter Jennessy. (April 2019)

"There's no such thing as a free lunch"

- Milton Friedman

<u>Chapter 3</u>

Factors

<u>Monday night 9:38 P.M. (Marathon deal finally closed)</u>

He looked at me and said, *"If it breaks, I'll fix it…"*

I replied and began to tell him how expensive the electronics are, how our labor rate was over $100 an hour, and how many of the diagnostics could only be performed at a selling dealer. Then he said, and I'm not lying, *"Well if it breaks, I'll just trade it in"*. (SMH).

Our customers should know better, but they often don't know, or understand the facts. So, what are the FACTS?

FACT # 1 – Most of your customers have very little savings available for emergencies, or unexpected hardships.

FACT # 2 – Most of your customers have very little idea about actual cost of ownership or reliability.

During times of economic prosperity people don't fear being sold, because spending a little extra money isn't a big deal when you have more than enough.

But today, Americans are finding they have less disposable income as inflation continues to grow. So, they will make what they perceive to be the most dollar-saving decision possible - based on their perception.

For some, the word *"No"* is like a lower payment coupon.

We must learn to intelligently discuss our products as it relates to saving people money if we want them to consider the benefits.

Many people don't realize exactly how much has changed in the last 20 years. Overall, inflation is up 48.9%[*] on basic goods and services, but over 250% for most vehicles.

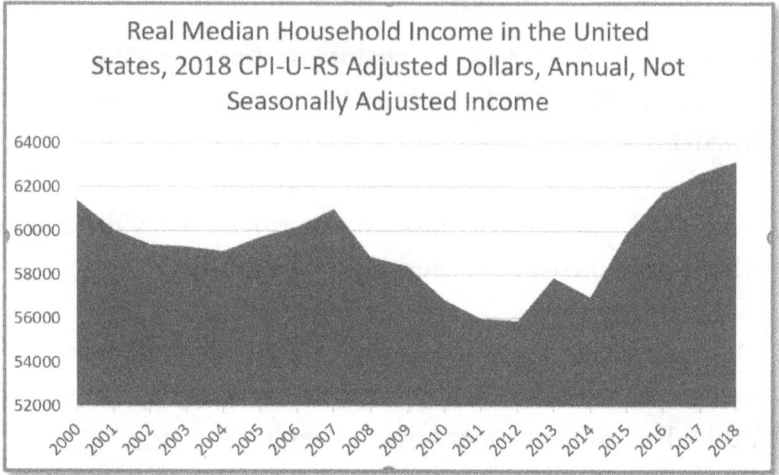

Real Median Household Income in the United States, 2018 CPI-U-RS Adjusted Dollars, Annual, Not Seasonally Adjusted Income

* The U.S. Labor Department's Bureau of Labor Statistics Consumer Price Index (CPI) - 2020
** Source: U.S. Census Bureau / fred.stlouisfed.org

That is right, inflation is up 48.9% and wages are only up 2.9%. Meanwhile, household income is stagnant. Barely moving from $61,399 in 2000, to $63,179 in 2018[**].

This presents more need than ever for customers to protect their budgets.

Most importantly for F&I Managers, the cavalier attitude people used to have with their money from 20 years ago is gone. People have changed. Customers today have no choice but to spend wisely or risk their quality of life.

HOW WE GOT HERE

From 1945 - 1965, Americans had the highest standard of living in the world. Our production and employment were high, and we made some of the best products on earth - largely because the rest of the world had been blown to pieces during World War II. We had a robust economy and people had lots of disposable income because everybody was making money. Additionally, inflation was capped by the Federal Reserve holding gold prices at $35 an ounce.

POSTMASTER: PLEASE POST IN A CONSPICUOUS PLACE. JAMES A. FARLEY, Postmaster General

UNDER EXECUTIVE ORDER OF THE PRESIDENT

Issued April 5, 1933

all persons are required to deliver

ON OR BEFORE MAY 1, 1933

all GOLD COIN, GOLD BULLION, AND GOLD CERTIFICATES now owned by them to a Federal Reserve Bank, branch or agency, or to any member bank of the Federal Reserve System.

Executive Order

Times were good, but in 1971, things began to change, and we've basically been in an economic decline since. The US Government decided to no longer convert dollars to gold - which had been the standard policy since 1933.

The American economy that worked very effectively in the 1930's, 40's, 50's and 60's, was beginning to unravel. The theme of the 70's became recessions and hardships. Nixon stepped down from the presidency, oil embargoes resulted in a lack of gasoline, and inflation began to outpace wages.

We had years of boom and bust, with inflation gradually outpacing household income, but it was manageable with the exception of a few recessions along the way. Many people found economic success by outworking others and out running inflation, until 2008.

In the 2008 recession, almost everyone struggled. The automotive industry was no exception. Many dealers didn't survive. While adjusting to the new economy, F&I managers began sharing with me that their word-tracks were becoming less effective. As if all customers had all become more cynical.

During that time, I felt that I needed to take a hard look at F&I in this new environment. So, I began taking occasional F&I spinning assignments in distinctively different environments (independent, highline and even recreational).

The basic enjoyment of working inside the dealership with customers again didn't hurt my spirits. I quickly discovered that the F&I training I had been taught in the early 1990's, and all the closes that I had been teaching to hundreds of F&I managers, were indeed, less effective. People were more cynical. I knew I would have to change if I wanted success.

Rather than presenting products, and trying to overcome objections all the time, I shifted my thinking.

For the first time in my career, I was having REAL conversations with my customers about their goals for the vehicle. I began to see products like Vehicle Service Contracts, GAP and Paint & Fab as ways to protect their budgets, instead of just ways for me to make gross.

Surprisingly, the gross was still there, but my attitude was completely different. My product count went way up, my chargebacks went way down. By not selling, I actually sold more.

Today, I understand why. I was focused on helping people, not selling people. The difference is paramount.

I didn't apply the 300% rule. Instead, I listened to people, I shared with people, I kept my process transparent and I ran my highest numbers ever.

THE TRUTH ABOUT PEOPLE

Mark was a very polished and persuasive Sales Manager for a large Toyota store. He averaged over $200,000 a year, in the same store - for the last 5 years. So, why was he broke?

The same reason most Americans are. Almost all of us engage in some pretty dysfunctional behavior and…
<u>Shhh, we don't want to talk about it</u>.

But it's true. It's our culture. The more money we make, the more money we spend. For most, more money means:

- Nicer clothes
- Nicer houses (and neighborhoods)
- Nicer cars
- More entertainment
- The newest smartphone
- More dinners out (at nicer restaurants)
- More money given to friends/family members with their own problems
- Etc…

But what it does <u>not</u> mean is more money set aside as savings, and rainy days. As a culture, we simply don't save.

That said, let me be clear… <u>THIS IS NOT CRITICISM</u>, it's only information. I will <u>not</u> criticize people for having nicer things or a better life.

Nicer things create a better quality of life, and sometimes we need that, myself included. We all need rewards for working hard, otherwise what is the point?

When we reward ourselves, we get a dose of Dopamine, the "feel-good" chemical. Our brains release it when we *feel* achievement or success. This is absolutely critical for our well-being.

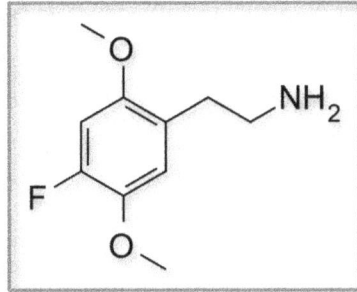

But we care about our loved ones too. So, we put in the hours to provide a better life for them. This behavior tells our brains to give us a dose of Oxytocin, the "warm-fuzzy" drug, that our brains release when we give to others. This is something we *feel* around teams, units, clubs, and strong families. It comes from belonging to something greater than yourself, and it is absolutely critical if you want to *feel* complete.

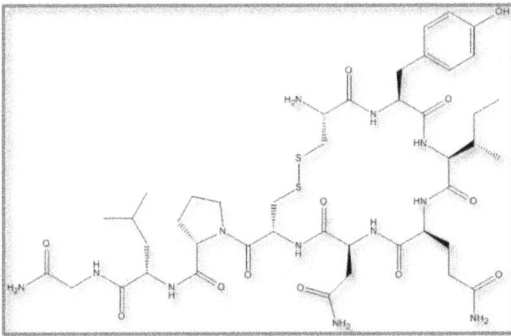

Missing either one of these chemical emotions can leave you unbalanced. For instance, you could have a fat bank account, yet still feeling empty inside. Alternatively, you could *feel* a deep devotion to family, friends or loved ones, but feeling like purpose or achievement are still missing.

We get Oxytocin when we help other people, and we get Dopamine when we help ourselves. We need both in balance for happiness. Too much or too little in either direction, and you can quickly become unbalanced and unhappy.

Let's say that I spend all my time "crushing it" everywhere I go. I go to the gym and "crush it". I go to work and "crush it". My bank account is "crushing it" and I am filled to the top with Dopamine. Could I still *feel* empty? Yes. I'll *feel* empty because I'm missing the Oxytocin that comes from feelings of love and team. We need that feeling of love and acceptance too. This ties directly into our interactions with customers.

Our goal should be finding the perfect balance of Dopamine and Oxytocin. This is the key to finding happiness in the box too. By focusing on making money for ourselves we create dopamine, and by focusing on solving problems for our customers we create Oxytocin. When we can find the ideal blend of these two chemicals, our lives improve.

In the box, we want to teach our customers about the products that help improve the quality of their lives and create The Best Ownership Experience™ – while getting paid nicely for providing those solutions. <u>This, in my opinion, is the essence of good F&I.</u>

Most people either reward themselves, or those they care about, as a result, there is very little money left over. This is a core reason why your customer doesn't want to give you any more of their money. It's likely their budget is already tight enough - regardless of their income.

You might think I'm speaking of lower income customers. I'm not. This is a similar story from the Buy Here/Pay Here lots all the way into the Porsche and Mercedes stores. Somewhere between 50-90% of the customers that walk through your door are on a "tight" budget.

In 2016, Bloomberg did a story on earners making over $150,000 a year and found that half of them are nearly broke (image). That they had very little saved and couldn't miss more than a couple weeks at work before they fell behind on their bills.

Save a Little, Make a Lot
A recent survey found that it's hardest for low income workers to save, but those making six figures aren't great at it either.

■ $0 ■ Less than $1,000 ■ $1,000-$4,999 ■ $5,000-$9,999 ■ $10,000+

Make Six Figures? There's a Decent Chance You've Got Almost Nothing in the Bank

The more you earn, the more you spend.

Bloomberg

This is just another example that as a culture we are so focused on "right now" that we don't plan for tomorrow.

Although we see a trend of more people earning over $100,000 a year, we must also pay attention to the uncomfortable truth that $100,000 worth of goods in the year 2000, would cost $149,000 today.

102

Americans' paychecks are bigger than 40 years ago, but their purchasing power has hardly budged

Average hourly wages in the U.S., seasonally adjusted

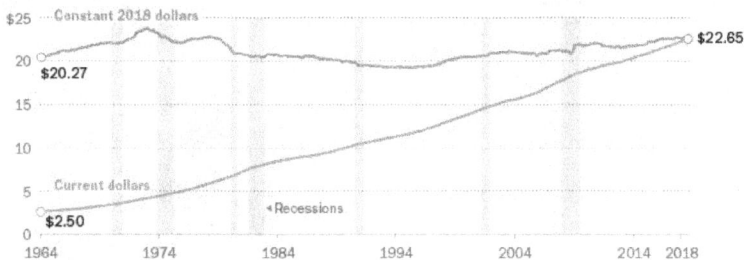

Note: Data for wages of production and non-supervisory employees on private non-farm payrolls. "Constant 2018 dollars" describes wages adjusted for inflation. "Current dollars" describes wages reported in the value of the currency when received. "Purchasing power" refers to the amount of goods or services that can be bought per unit of currency.
Source: U.S. Bureau of Labor Statistics.

PEW RESEARCH CENTER

Wages are well below where they should be relative to advances in automotive inflation. And no relief is coming.

When wages rise, the stock market falls. This is because corporations recognize that higher wages = lower profits. So, prices must go up again - and the cycle continues.

Many families have been dealing with tight budgets for a long time now. Because money is tighter now many people are focused on *"not getting sold"*. Even when products like Pre-Paid Maintenance can help them save money and have better control over their budgets, some people will still say *"No"*.

That said, money will become even tighter if trends continue. The result will inevitably be more customers arguing over payments, or surrendering to longer terms.

103

WILLPOWER AND MARSHMALLOWS

In the 1960's, a group of young children were part of a study on patience and deferring rewards for greater gain – or so they thought. (The study was actually about "framing".)

Researchers would bring each child into a room, then tell the child, *"This is your marshmallow. You can eat it anytime you like, but if you're willing to wait until I come back, I'll give you another marshmallow"*.

For some children, the researcher would walk out and within seconds the marshmallow was gone, eaten and an empty plate was all that remained.

For others, they fought to control themselves. They'd sniff it. They'd lick it. They'd hold it and talk to themselves about the dilemma they were facing.

Yet, there were a few that understood the goal clearly;
defer the instant gratification now for a greater reward later.

These are the people you don't have to sell. They are
already listening, and forming judgments and opinions
based on data. They are making assessments of your
character. While waiting for the data on your products.
But the deferred gratification group is getting smaller.

Usually, we find ourselves sitting across from customers
that are completely concerned about one thing. Getting the
"lowest payment" today, and not giving any consideration
to the "best payment", or the payment that solves
tomorrow's problems.

THE LOWEST PAYMENT CONUNDRUM

Everyone wants the "lowest payment", right? How do we get there? By stretching out the term and skipping all the financial protection options. Probably not a good idea. This sets the customer up for higher finance charges, additional negative equity, and potential economic hardships.

What is the "best payment"?

It is the payment that is designed to create equity and prevent economic hardship. An example of the "best payment" would be protecting themselves by adopting solutions for mechanical breakdowns, cost effective servicing, keeping their vehicle's appearance intact, and eliminating gaps in insurance coverage.

Having the "best payment" simply means making intelligent choices. Choices that will create the Best Ownership Experience™ for your customer.

Sometimes this can be difficult. Sometimes your customers are so focused on the "lowest payment" that they'll tune out anything you say about products. Sometimes they fear the "best payment" when they should actually fear a breakdown, a need for GAP, or just negative equity because these types of events are far more traumatic than finding an extra $40 or $50 a month for protection.

Recently, the CEO of a nationally known, publicly traded lender told me this, *"Many of our customers have less than $400 in emergency savings"*. This is disturbing and it's not just subprime, its everywhere, even customers shopping in high-line stores have little savings.

Some of you guys can relate. I often hear from F&I managers looking for new jobs and they'll say, *"I need to make at least $12K a month or it's not worth getting out of bed"*. But, they too have very little saved, then they go on to explain that they really need to get back to work right away, or else.

We often want the best of everything, and we want it now - without considering the true cost. That is why credit card companies are so profitable. It's also why customers skip important products like extended service contracts and gap insurance, only to find out later that a single repair or GAP claim can economically devastate them. Sometimes to the point where their rent or mortgage payments are in jeopardy.

One unfortunate automotive event could ruin their credit for years. Even if they're able to use a credit card to finance their way through the current problem, it's not a quality solution. They could easily pay twice as much for a repair over time, assuming they paid a fair price for the repair. (image next page)

An air conditioner repair example:

Air Conditioner Compressor			TRUE
Parts	$	877.92	COST
Labor (3.5 hrs)	$	393.88	**$2917**
Misc Supplies & Fees	$	125.79	
Total	$	**1,397.59**	
Paying by credit card? Add $1519 in interest over 146 months			

In the Air Compressor example, we see the initial cost of $1,397.59 is more than doubled to a true cost of $2,917 after interest is charged by the credit card provider.

THE TRUTH ABOUT VEHICLES

We are in exceptional times. Throughout all human history, no one has ever owned anything quite like a modern car. Making all the pieces work together is an amazing achievement. This is the result of millions of human labor hours.

6'0" Adult

Accordingly, vehicles today have more computer code <CODE> than almost anything else ever made. More than smartphones, computers, the space shuttle, fighter jets, even The Hadron Collider (image above) - we use for splitting atoms.

Nothing else we own is like a modern car.

What is a car exactly? It's just a metal cage with a bunch of parts from all over the world working together to help us travel. It is also likely to be the most technologically advanced thing that you, or I, will ever own.

109

It is a machine powered by fire. It's forced to operate in incredibly hot and cold climates. Designed to provide safety, security, and reliability – all while hitting potholes at 60MPH.

Many of today's vehicles have upwards of one-hundred million (100,000,000) lines of <CODE> making sure each of the 50-200 on-board computers are working.

Many of these computers are "SYSTEM CRITICAL" for the safety and proper operation of the vehicle. If they fail, it could mean a failure to launch the airbags or deploy ABS, on the super important side - or the inability to play your favorite song on the less significant side.

When you think about it, this technology is why we buy newer cars, isn't it?

In short, a car is an amazing accomplishment. Yet some of your customers expect them to <u>always</u> operate perfectly. Why? Is expecting "flawless reliability" a reasonable belief? I'm just going to say this, and I'm sorry, but…All cars will eventually breakdown. It's true. Given enough time, parts will break, they will malfunction, and they will fail. It's that simple.

That said, some cars are better than others. Let's explore why…

What do most corporations do? Pursue profit of course. This is their primary objective.

Yes, they may wish to innovate, or they may have some noble philosophical goals at their core. But ultimately, they must create profit for shareholders or face management turnover. Businesses require profits to remain in business, and CEO's must generate profits to keep their jobs.

Quarterly reports, not ethics, determine CEO longevity in most cases. Not that CEO's are bad, but they have a responsibility to create profit and effectively compete against their competitors.

This is not a secret.

It's not as if the manufacturer even has a choice in the matter. It's an incredibility competitive marketplace. Revenue goals must be hit and it's not easy to raise prices without losing customers. Very few automakers have a niche demographic of people with unlimited income to spend. For everyone else, automakers try to balance manufacturing costs, maintain profit margins, and offer a product that is still priced competitive in the marketplace. So, they have third party companies bid on building the parts they need.

Of course, the third-party companies are also working on tight margins. Afterall, they had to be the lowest bidder to win the contract. They also needed to provide a quality part or risk harming the brand's reputation. This is not always possible, and it is the main reason your customers can benefit from having a quality Vehicle Service Contract.

Any part can fail, regardless of the brand on the front of the vehicle. Sometimes, an automaker will switch a part when they see the performance of that part diminishing too quickly. For owners of these cars, they'll soon be on their own with a part that wasn't known to be inferior at the time the manufacturer selected it.

Test it below ⬇

Imagine for a moment that you work for a major automotive manufacturer that sells a million units a year. You have found a way to save $.25 on each valve stem. This would save the company $100,000. Would you do it?

If you answered "Yes", it's probably because your payplan provides incentives for you to create a profit.

Now, imagine if instead of just valve stems, you were able to negotiate lower costs for almost every single part on the car?

That basically by only building the engine, transmission, frame & body, and outsourcing everything else out to third-party companies, your company would save $1000 per unit and gross an additional Billion Dollars (1,000,000,000.00) a year. How much incentive would a Billion dollars a year provide?

Common third-party parts are:

Climate control   Engine cooling parts
Suspension parts   Brake systems
Steering parts   Wheels
Fuel systems   Passenger restraint systems
Audio and telematics   Exhaust
Etc.

FOLLOW THE MONEY

Parts fail. This is why we have auto parts stores in every town. This is also why auto parts stores are thriving.

If you invested $1 dollar in the Dow Jones Industrials (DJI) or the NASDAQ Composite Index in January 2010, your dollar would be worth between $2.66-$3.80 in January 2020 (pre-corona).

But, if you invested that same dollar in auto parts providers such as AutoZone (AZO) or O'Reilly (ORLY) your dollar would be worth between $6.82-$10.78. These auto parts companies have out-performed the general market by nearly 3-to-1.

Would this kind of growth be possible if vehicles didn't incur breakdowns? No.

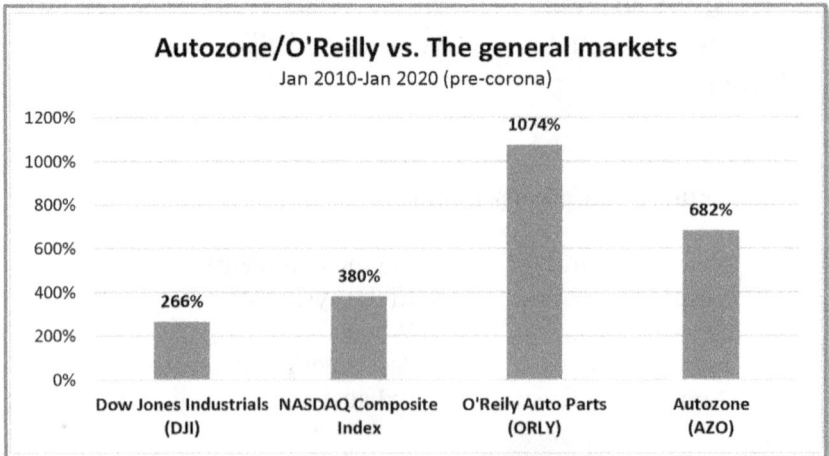

Autozone/O'Reilly vs. The general markets
Jan 2010-Jan 2020 (pre-corona)

If you're still not sure vehicles breakdown, check the 2020 JD Power Dependability study (next page). Nearly every vehicle made had some problem within the first three years. Genesis was the best with 89 problems per 100 vehicles and the worst had over 200 problems per 100 vehicles manufactured.

That said, automakers know with relative certainty, how their vehicles are likely to perform, and then they provide their factory warranty coverage with that in mind. This is why the Basic (Bumper-to-bumper) warranty isn't very long on most cars.

Of course, occasionally we see companies like Chrysler (1997 & 2003), or Volkswagen (2018), offer longer warranties to stimulate sales. Even then, the majority of the coverage is only on the engine and transmission, not on the third-party parts.

J.D. Power
2020 U.S. Vehicle Dependability Study[SM]

Brand Ranking

Problems per 100 (PP100)

Brand	PP100
Genesis	89
Lexus	100
Buick	103
Porsche	104
Toyota	113
Volkswagen	116
Lincoln	119
BMW	123
Chevrolet	123
Ford	126
Mazda	130
Cadillac	131
Hyundai	132
Kia	132
Industry Average	134
Audi	136
Nissan	136
Acura	139
Honda	139
Ram	140
Mitsubishi	146
MINI	147
Mercedes-Benz	152
Subaru	154
Infiniti	155
Dodge	158
Jeep	159
Fiat	160
GMC	162
Volvo	185
Jaguar	186
Chrysler	214
Land Rover	220

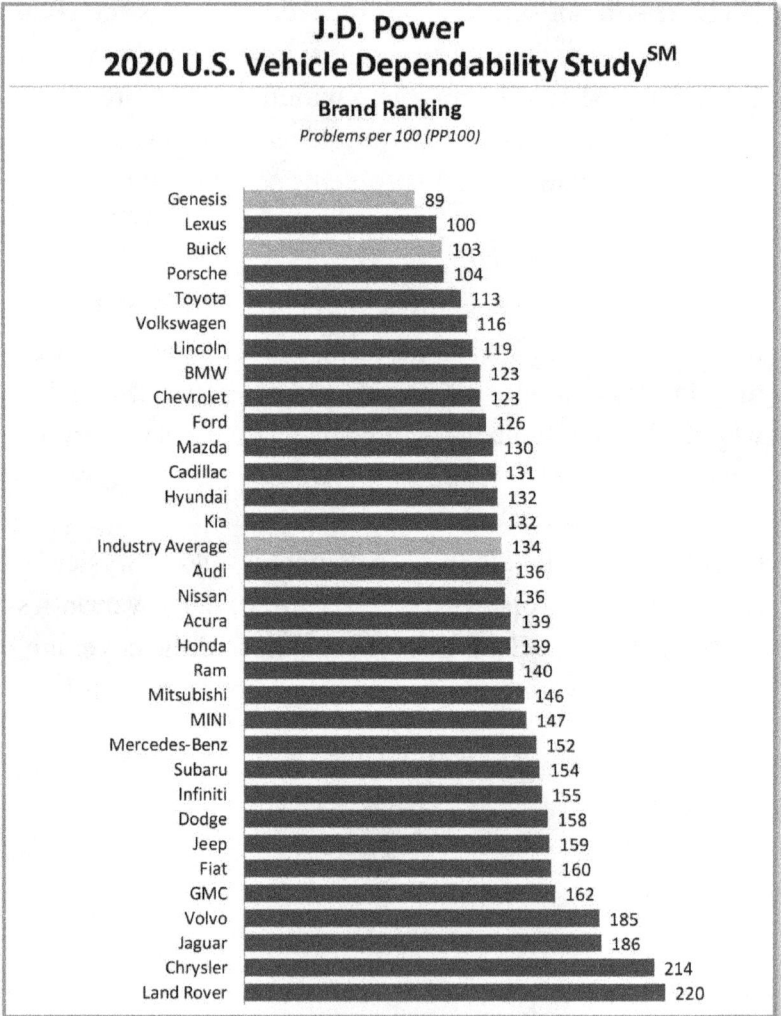

Source: J.D. Power 2020 U.S. Vehicle Dependability Study[SM]

DO YOUR CUSTOMERS ACTUALLY *NEED* COVERAGE?

Does your customer actually need a VSC, GAP or Paint protection? To figure this out, we have to define exactly what the word need means to each of us.

What exactly does "need" mean to you?

In our customer's world, "need" might mean the customer *needs* a VSC because they're likely to experience a breakdown.

Another customer might *need* a VSC because they have no disposable income left over.

Another customer might *need* a VSC because at this point in their life they can afford comfort and peace of mind.

Conversely, another customer may just *need* to "win" in the negotiation. When I say win, I mean leave the car dealership without getting "hurt" as they see it. Not being sold a bill of goods is what they *feel* they *need* more than the protection of the product or service that you're offering them.

Its emotional, not logical, but it's still a *need*.

WHAT YOUR CUSTOMERS ACTUALLY *NEED*

Every year, The American Automotive Association (AAA), completes a report on the average cost of ownership and operation of vehicles. They consider 7 different factors:

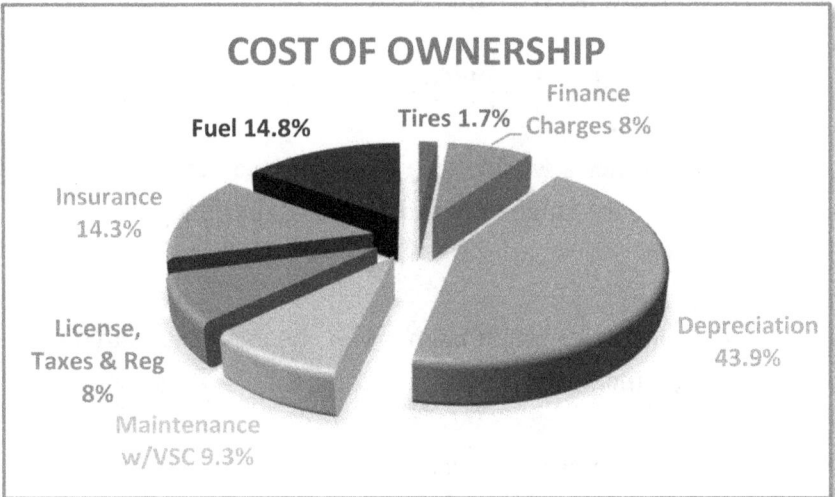

COST OF OWNERSHIP

- Fuel 14.8%
- Tires 1.7%
- Finance Charges 8%
- Insurance 14.3%
- License, Taxes & Reg 8%
- Maintenance w/VSC 9.3%
- Depreciation 43.9%

While we cannot assist with things like Fuel, License, Taxes or Insurance costs, we can have some influence on Vehicle Deprecation, Maintenance, Repairs, Tires and Finance Charges.

These costs represent **62.9%** of the overall cost of ownership and can be reduced through products like Vehicle Service Contracts, Maintenance Plans, Paint & Fabric Protection, Cosmetic Wheel Protection, Key Fob Protection, and even more attractive financing options.

Test it below

Do products really help?

Imagine a car in excellent condition, with perfect paint and perfect interior. Free of repairs with plenty of warranty in place. It has a solid history of all its maintenance.

Is it worth more than a vehicle in average condition with average wear?

Keeping the car perfect adds value, not only economically, but it also adds enjoyment, prestige, and works to reduce people's anxiety.

FAKE NEWS

Dave Ramsey says, *"Skip the protection"*. This is also what the so called "experts" on TV say too, but *they* don't bring any data. Instead, *they* only have opinions, and *they* are not actually risk experts.

Actuaries and underwriters are where I get my data. People on TV are really just experts in the entertainment business. Their job is really to attract and keep viewers. Period. If the viewers stop watching, the "so-called experts" become unemployed.

No one really regulates what is and isn't true. TV shows levy opinions, but don't supply hard data. No one discusses actuarial rates or loss ratios for vehicles and insurance products, so instead they just make statements of opinion.

The media, similar to their advertisers have very little restriction on what cannot be said or claimed. So, often "opinions" are presented as facts, just like cigarettes and sugar once were.

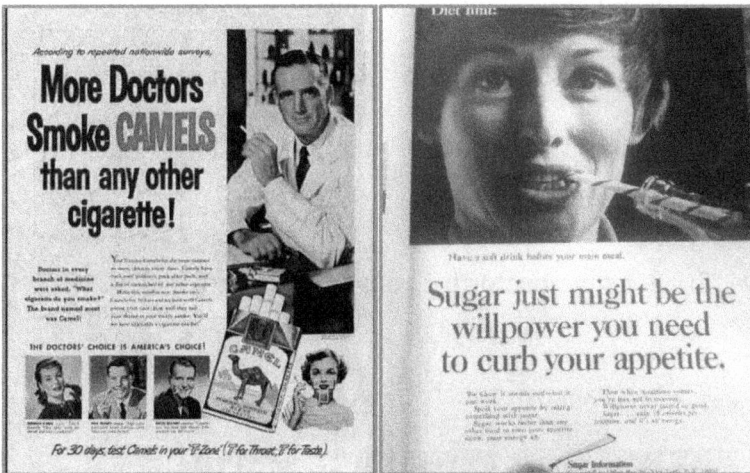

The "experts" haven't been in the insurance business for over two decades, but I have. I worked for, and with some of the largest companies in the world. I understand risk and what it takes to build a vehicle service contract program from the ground up.

That said, I always buy VSC coverage on my vehicles. On furniture, cell phones, and etc. too. I like to have the real "experts" manage my risk.

I had 9 claims over the last few years. Maybe I'm unlucky. Still, when something goes wrong, it's rare that it's a real problem.

Claims paid:

1. New iPhone. Covered by Apple care.

2. O2 sensor. Covered by my VSC.

3. Front strut. Covered by my VSC.

4. Broken shifter cable. Covered by my VSC.

5. Clutch sensor. Covered by my VSC.

6. Water pump. Covered by my VSC.

7. Strut connector for convertible top. Covered by VSC.

8. Stain on my couch. Covered by Guardsman.

9. New printer. Covered by SquareTrade.

In return I received:

1. No major out of pocket expenses.

2. No major loss of time.

3. No major inconvenience.

The thing I'm looking for when I consider insurance is "what makes sense". If it's a quality program, I add it.

Side note: I also pay retail pricing every time on my automotive products, and even though I could buy at cost, I don't. I want to have the same experience that my customer has, and I also want to support F&I profitability.

Test it below

Imagine you are a professional mechanic and your car breaks down. Yes, you could fix it, but you shouldn't.

Here's why... Good mechanics work quickly. If a repair guide (image) says a job should take 1 hour, a master mechanic can finish it a lot faster. He can earn 2, 3, maybe even 4 hours of "labor time" for each actual hour of real time.

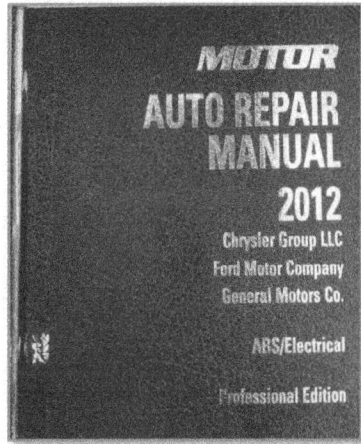

In short, he'll lose a chunk of his own income by working on his own car.

For perspective, consider another profession:

If barber "A" averages 1 cut per hour and barber "B" can complete 3 haircuts in an hour, who makes more money? This is basically the same thing.

For the rest of us, the garage will still charge us whatever amount the labor guide says - regardless of how many actual hours the mechanic takes to complete the repair.

Also, let's not forget that there are many different labor guides and repair shops will always use what benefits them.

> **<u>Common labor guides are:</u>**
> **ALLDATA**
> **MOTOR**
> **MITCHELL**
> **CHILTON**

I don't know about you, but I'm experienced, and I don't know how to tell if the shop is being honest on labor hours, or parts pricing, without doing some research. I also don't want to haggle with multiple mechanics and garages to try and find the best deal in town.

So, I buy a quality VSC on every car I purchase and let the insurance company "baby sit" the repair facility for me, while I drive away in a loaner.

These are realities that the "so-called experts" on TV never mention. They never mention that even the smallest failure could take hours to repair, and cost thousands of dollars. They never mention reliability varies by make and model. They never mention labor guides. They never mention anything about fair pricing from the mechanic.

But, if you want a second opinion, ask any mechanic how long it would take to diagnose a short in the wiring harness.

(Good luck getting a precise answer)

The Bentley Bentayga wiring harness.

Me, holding the wiring harness
for a 2017 Honda Accord.

Watch your thoughts; they become words.
Watch your words; they become actions.
Watch your actions; they become habit.
Watch your habits; they become character.
Watch your character; it becomes your
destiny."

- **Lao Tzu**

<u>Chapter 4</u>

Purpose

<u>Thursday afternoon 3:38 P.M. (Recontract)</u>

He looked at me and said, *"No, thank you"*. This was a big problem because I forgot my ethics at the door...

The desk miscalculated the tag fees on his lease, which left some "leg" in the payment. I skipped my normal process completely. Instead of transparency and decency, I tried to "trick" my way into a quick product sale. I said, *"By the way, our Road Hazard Package is only an extra $3.00 month, sound good?"*. Thinking he would just agree, but he didn't.

His "trust alarm" was going off and for good reason. I tried again, hoping to convey the value this time, but no luck. After the third try he said, *"I guess I can't have the car if I don't buy it, so fine, I'll take it. May I just have the car so I can go home please?"*

This whole situation was super embarrassing. Then, his deal wouldn't fund as contracted. Two days later, I was sitting with him again for the recon. Convicted for my bad act, twice.

That was a very long time ago, but it was also the last time I wasn't completely transparent with a customer. Today, I recognize the only way that customer would have bought was after trust was established, and all I did was destroy it.

Lesson learned.

FINDING PURPOSE

On January 15th, 2009, US Airways flight 1549 had to make an emergency landing shortly after departing LaGuardia International Airport, in New York. The aircraft, captained by Chesley "Sully" Sullenberger, encountered a flock of Canadian geese that flew into both engines, and caused a catastrophic failure.

He was flying over the city of Manhattan, which made it impossible to land and he was too far from the local airports. His only choice was to land the plane in the Hudson river.

US Airways Flight 1549
January 15, 2009

His "Thinking and Feeling Self" were displayed over the PA for his passengers as they feared for their lives. Yet, they heard his voice over the PA and felt some level of trust. This was not a man in a state of panic. He was calm while explaining the process of what was about to happen.

Sully felt fear just like anyone would, but his purpose gave him strength. Had he quit; all would have died. But he didn't. As a result, all 155 "souls" survived.

What is your purpose? Making money for the sake of having money isn't enough. What is your why?

Money is a tool for bigger things. We must dig deeper and find the underlying purpose for why we want the money.

Usually, we find our sacrifices of long hours and late nights have something very meaningful at their root. We must get in touch with those reasons if we hope to have the courage to be truly transparent with our customers.

STORYTELLING

We believe the story we've been told about money's value and purpose our whole lives. That story is consistently evolving and eventually we all learn that money isn't the key to happiness. It is a tool that can bring some happiness, but it is far from guaranteed. And we absolutely know that without enough money we will suffer. We absolutely understand the bank demands it for our homes and car loans. The grocery store demands it for the food we need.

Your customer is working with these thoughts when you're asking them for their money. They likely understand the absolute truth that if they waste money, they will have less groceries in the refrigerator. That is pretty easy math, and it's absolute.

But, what about the intrinsic value. Their belief in money. That is still "just a story". Just like the story that "you're just another salesperson". So, tell a new story. One where you share experiences of how you helped other customers through true stories.

If you don't have any, get to work. Get involved. Get personal. This is what builds your authenticity. The more real you are, the more people will trust your telling the truth.

Storytelling is very powerful. I can convert $50 a month into peace of mind. Safety. Comfort. It can help remedy stress… But only if the customer believes it gives those things.

So, instead of trying to use a slick word track designed to manipulate them into being scared, tell your true stories of how people have been helped because of you. The feeling of the transaction will change in a positive direction.

According to Rational Choice Theory, humans always work in their own best interests. Based on beliefs, they make decisions they *feel* are in their best interests.

If I am your customer and I *feel* that you are trying to sell me something I don't need, or that you're trying to rip me off, then any data you share with me will become irrelevant.

I will say "no" and each time you attempt to overcome my objection, I will retreat more into my "fight or flight" responses. This is why we must not focus on closing.

Instead, we must focus on telling the truth. Regardless of what that means. Because over time, the *"feeling"* people get from you will be a much more powerful closing tool than a word-track.

Test it below ⬇

A customer asks you "Do I have to decide today?"

From our very own selfish perspective, we want to say *"yes"* (even if it's not true). We might say *"no"*, but then begin "selling" on all the reasons why they should buy today. Not because we care, but because we're thinking of our PVR, our Penetration, our Paycheck. But for the customer this situation only adds pressure, or worse, fear.

What if instead we do the right thing immediately. We're honest and say *"no"*. Counterintuitive? Yes. But follow me for a moment…

Imagine you're the customer buying a vehicle. You ask me *"must I buy it today?"* and my answer causes you to *feel* unsure about the purchase. You begin to slow down. You begin to withdraw trust.

But if I come across completely honest, you can relax. Maybe you'll say *"no"* to the VSC right now. That's ok. I might leave a brochure or the menu on the desk, but I don't push.

Then a couple minutes later, you ask a question about the coverage. Boom! Now, I begin telling you some <u>real</u> stories. The sale occurs and you *feel* good about the products and *feel* good about our experience together.

THE ART OF F&I

You could look at your job like you're an insignificant cog in the machine, or… you could look at it like you are a necessary part of an engine.

This is a choice. The behaviors that you bring to work will echo through the culture of your dealership, and eventually through the network that you touch in your community.

Behaviors like character, leadership, wisdom, doggedness and self-discipline. Showing that you can be trusted to do the right thing. This is something that we must bring to work, and we must expand to become our core purpose.

In short; we must agree to always do the right thing, regardless where it leaves us.

The economics of always doing the right thing may not be as attractive on one single deal, but over the week, the month, the year, or your whole business career, we can see the economics are largely in our favor once we always opt to do the right thing.

To begin with, once people can learn to trust us, there's less negotiation. For this to occur, we must let go of the outcome....

To be blunt. We must stop our focus on overcoming objections. But first, we must quit behaving in ways that create those objections in the first place.

We must show people that we are REAL. We must demonstrate that our purpose is about helping them have a good experience. Of course, we also have a purpose of revenue generation, but so does almost everyone else, working anywhere, for any type of business. Most businesses only exist because they have found a way to make a profit. The need to make profit is a given, adjusting margins accordingly to create the proper culture is optional.

Our foremost goal, or focus, needs to be on creating positive experiences for our customers and co-workers alike. Then building our growth and profit strategies around those behaviors.

When we only focus on profit, everyone tends to suffer. When we focus on creating a quality experience for all parties, it's different. Consider a company like Disney. They are selling an excellent experience and building price around the cost to provide that experience.

Being customer focused sounds easy, but there's a grey area. Many dealers jump deeply into the customer experience. They commit, but it's doesn't help their bottom line. Why?

Wrong focus. We can't simply focus on our customers. They're often irrational, and they're also trying to minimize our profit. Because years of dysfunctional sales practices have led to dysfunctional consumer behaviors.

We need to rein this in. The more professional we are, the more ethical we are, the less dysfunctional the process will be; but it starts with us.

F&I managers need to grow into the role of overseer for ethics and standards. Yes, sales of F&I products are still important. They must take second place to building a sustainable culture of excellence within your store.

Most F&I managers are subjected to about 1 week of training on menu presentation and overcoming objections, but it's not deep learning. As a result, it becomes impossible to create a culture of excellence in the store.

Because of this situation they often just become clerks, they obey the desk, and then they burnout. This is a huge problem. But the remedy is finding purpose.

CUI BONO

When we begin the interaction with our customers, we are forming a relationship and if your idea of a relationship is only 30-45 minutes, your behavior will reflect it. If your conversation is only about completing a transaction, it will be different than when you're making a friend. This will *feel* completely different to the customer.

There are endless ways to let your customers know they are more than another transaction to you. Let's build a relationship with our customers. One where if you and the customer met in the future someday, it would *feel* positive. A transaction where both parties win. This is our goal, but it takes real commitment to find a win/win.

The first problem will be time. The thing about F&I is that nothing happens for 5 hours and then 3 deals close within 30 minutes of each other. You will quickly be reminded, by everyone in the building, that another customer is waiting. It may seem impossible to create a relationship in only a few minutes, but it happens all the time.

In order for it to occur, we must create trust. We must become more than a part of the transaction to them. In order to have a win/win, we must have a two-way street.

It is of paramount importance that you know what you hope to accomplish, before you meet them.

138

Ask yourself who benefits? Cui Bono?

Are we looking for a transaction where we all parties win and leave each other with feelings of respect?

I must ask myself *"Who benefits in this deal?"* and get my intent customer focused. I only have one chance to make a first impression that inspires them to relax and communicate with me.

Am I focused on profit? Of course, it would be irresponsible not to be, but I hope to find the sweet spot where a balance occurs. A transaction where revenue goals are achieved, and CSI excels.

Can we add efficiency and satisfaction?

Can we have a more predictable bottom line?

Absolutely.

Ultimately, at the end of the transaction. The customer should *feel* like, *"Yeah, I'd buy here again"*

A perfect transaction leaves feeling of respect, appreciation, and at its very best... bonding friendships.

AUTHENTICITY

A large part of belief comes from being authentic... But what you are authentic about also matters?

If I am authentically and unapologetically a jerk, then only a small percentage of people will warm up to me. If I'm authentically "smug" or "too good" for those around me, even more people will think I'm a jerk.

Our goal must be to find the place in between. A place where we live in harmony with our goals. Where we find the internal discipline to live accordingly with our values and demonstrate external empathy and *feel* for people when they try to find their authentic self but fail.

Let's discuss your values…

Do you <u>always</u> live in exact harmony with your principles? No?! It's ok, no one is perfect. But if we hope to have self-esteem, or to even like ourselves when we look in the mirror, we must be on that journey. We must try.

When we don't even try, we begin to disrespect ourselves. Over time, we *feel* shame. Sometimes we seek an escape through binging on TV, Social Media, Gaming, or more seriously, alcohol, drugs, bad food choices, etc. We seek a source of dopamine that temporarily makes us *feel* a little less suffering, but it doesn't actually fix the problem.

Beyond the box, we must try to live according to our principles in our personal lives too. Our behaviors in our everyday lives inspire self-trust, and as a result, we learn to love ourselves a little more.

In short, you must be the best version of yourself that you can be.

It matters. People _feel_ it… and when other people can't _feel_ it, there will be economic consequences.

YOU 2.0

Finding happiness and success require a process. Here are 10 areas, built on Stoic principles, that you can develop to ensure that you're always improving:

Your purpose... Your purpose is in front of you. This means make the most of the present. Today. Life is short. The Past is no longer within our control and the Future is not guaranteed. So, we must make the most of now.

Ask yourself, "How can I make the most out of my time and circumstances?"

Your value... We exist for the sake of one another. We all have unique gifts and talents. Use them to create value for others that need you.

Ask yourself, "What am I good at, who can I help with my skills, knowledge or talents, and what do people need?"

Your passion... The car business is not for everyone. If you don't love it what are the chances you're going to enjoy staying in it or even excelling at it? If it's not your calling, or if other passions are always calling you away, you must make some adjustments to suit those passions.

Ask yourself, "What efforts am I making in areas that make me happy?"

Your urgency... Once we begin doing what we love we become obsessed. Not good at your passion yet, so what, do it anyway. Every opportunity. Create easy goals and keep after them. A little at a time.

Ask yourself, "What can I do today to get closer to my ideal life?"

Your strength... Just don't quit. Eventually you will have successes. Sometimes we hit roadblocks and that is ok. Show up everyday and do what you can.

Ask yourself, "What would happen if I tried to accomplish at least one of my goals every single day?"

Your fear... You get what you focus on. Worrying about negative things creates negative focus. Most of life is out of our control anyway, so we must focus on the things that we can control.

Ask yourself, "Is this the best place to focus my thoughts or my energy? Or could I focus them in more positive areas?"

Your heroes... Finding someone that has already walked the path to their potential or overcame their weaknesses is helpful for motivating us to do the same.

Ask yourself, "Who do I admire or respect and why?"

Your circle... Everyone's opinions vary, but none walk in your shoes. Their experiences in life differ from yours and while they may mean well, it can still be a disruption towards achieving your goals.

Ask yourself, "Where is this negativity coming from and what are they trying to achieve?"

Your challenges... Whatever is holding you from living the life you seek is the way. Go address it, head on, and get to the other side of whatever is holding you back.

Ask yourself, "How could my life improve if I could remedy this one problem?"

Your perseverance... Life goes on. As you achieve goals, new desires and obstacles will await you. The process of working through problems is never ending, but your ability to solve problems will continue to improve as long as you live.

Ask yourself, "Do I need a new purpose and what around me is good reason for my time and efforts?"

S.O.S. *(Same old story)*

People always do one of the following three things:

1) They pick packages – We know what to do when they pick a package, right? WE PRINT!!!

2) They ask questions – Do we know how to answer all their questions? I hope so… This is an opportunity for you to gain trust. Questions are opportunities, embrace them.

3) They object. - What if they object? Often their objection is not based on good data.

For instance, a customer that says *"no"* before they even see the cost, or the coverage, of the product or package you're offering isn't saying *"no"* to the product. They are saying *"no"* to you.

If they don't trust us, the dealership or the product, it's going to be a challenge. If they had a negative past car buying experience, or maybe their friends/family have told them horror stories about a dealership, this can make the transaction more difficult for sure, but this is not necessarily a problem.

It is an opportunity to create trust. So, let's drill down a little into the behaviors of creating trust…

If I do not trust you… or I think you're trying to take advantage of me, I'm not going to buy anything from you.

If I do not trust you… I will feed you irrational responses every time you try and close me.

If I do not trust you… you may wear me down long enough to get my signature, so I can go home. But I will cancel as soon as I have an opportunity.

As a finance manager, if we want to achieve above average results, we must learn to communicate, and we must learn to operate with a spirit of a win-win. People can *feel* the difference when you're only there for yourself.

Do you frame lack of trust as a threat, or as an opportunity?

<u>If your trying to take advantage of someone, then lack of trust is a deal killer, but if you're intent is about helping them, then you can fearlessly go anywhere in the conversation.</u>

What your customer is looking for is two-fold. They are looking for you to show them your character, and your competency. They want to know you are trying to treat them fairly, and you know how to create a positive experience for them.

We must show them our character and our competency if we hope to communicate with them. If we fail, then they will dismiss us and our products.

We show our character by being genuine and discussing products based on their agenda. This is about helping people solve problems.

We also show our competency by having a deep understanding of exactly how our products work and how they will solve problems for our customers.

When working with our customers, we must be in the room - not just in our heads. We begin by listening deeply, without a time or profit agenda. We listen. We watch. We learn how to behave in a helping and caring manner. We remember that we are here to serve. We are here to create a positive experience.

That is our job, and it is also the most profitable process.

Test it below

Imagine you're talking with a doctor or a lawyer. How important is clear communication?

How important is it that they care about your results? If they treat you like just another transaction, how would that make you *feel*?

It's super important we understand our intent, or what we hope to create, during the short relationship with them.

What is your intent? To make a profit. Of course, that is being responsible for good business, but you must compartmentalize your desire here. You must put the customer first.

If that means a 15-minute transaction with no products, then let's get to it. Let's get to the next customer while they're still excited. Why don't we push here?

One reason; there's no trust yet.

Imagine you don't know me, and I decide you need to listen to my political opinions, and if you disagree, I'm going to keep pushing. How well is this going to work out for me?

Same thing with your opinion about F&I products.

If they believe in "not getting ripped off", and you haven't demonstrated your intentions are about helping them yet, they will not listen.

They will tune you out.

They will argue.

They will push the menu back.

Or maybe they'll just ask, *"Can I buy it later?"*

Our only hope is to make sure our intent is focused on them from the beginning. We must genuinely want the transaction to be easy and helpful. We must genuinely want them to leave feeling good about our time together. Anything else is going to be a battle.

"I can't think the music, but I can feel it"

- Featherfoot

A CULTURE OF EXCELLENCE

Ever stay at the Four Seasons? The staff practices making the EXPERIENCE exceptional for their guests. They slow down, they authentically make eye contact, attempt to help, solve problems, or just listen. Yes, it costs more to stay there compared with other hotels, but the experience is incredibly different than those hotels.

They focus on creating a "positive experience" while we often focus on "maximizing profits in the shortest time possible". There is a profound difference.

Now imagine yourself slowing down and demonstrating that same professionalism, and authentic care, towards the customer. Perhaps even making their interaction with you the best part of their day.

Why does this matter?

People begin making decisions about your trustworthiness the moment they meet you. And I promise if you don't believe you're there to help them, it's going to be hard to inspire your customer to believe you.

Test it below ⬇

Imagine yourself in a meeting with a fitness coach. The coach is completely out of shape. He seems unsure about how you're going to achieve the results you seek. Do you move forward and hire him? No? Why not?

Imagine the same thing in the box. You're buying a car and you *feel* like something is off. The F&I manager doesn't look organized or you notice the lack of professionalism and begin feeling some uncertainty.

You want a VSC and begin to ask questions about the coverage, but the answers are vague. All his answers are preceded or followed by the words, *"I think..."* or *"Should be fine..."*, or other non-committal phrases.

Maybe, instead, he sounds scripted or canned. The "information overload" attempt, filled with vague statements and irrelevant information. It's obviously inauthentic, as if the F&I manager would say anything to sell you. Do you move forward?

As previously discussed, there is a dynamic in play here that is incredibly important.

You, me, anybody, in any transaction ever, is working with two different sets of data, Thoughts & Feelings. They compete with each other, but ultimately Feelings will win.

Feelings, not Thoughts, buy the car, or the service contract, or the gap coverage, or the chemical package, or for that matter, anything. The "Feeling self" wants what it wants. And the "Thinking self" justifies what the "Feeling self" has already decided on.

If I ask you for directions or instructions, my head or "Thinking self" will be involved, but...

If I ask you to listen as I play my favorite song, your gut or your "Feeling Self" will be engaged, and you'll begin making judgments and trust assessments about me.

"Between stimulus and response there is a space. In that space is our power to choose our response. In our response lies our growth and freedom"

- Viktor Frankl

Chapter 5

Final thoughts

In order to help people "help themselves", you'll need to communicate effectively. But, engaging people with new and sometimes uncomfortable information requires tact.

It requires you to have the ability to say, **"HARD THINGS"** in a very **"soft way"**. You can do this by focusing your intent on helping them. If the product you're proposing is a good idea, gently discuss the reasons they will benefit from having it, and then, the problems it will solve.

Here are two examples of the same conversation. Notice the key words that have been changed:

"Most customers want to have a great experience; I suspect that you do too. When I say great experience, I mean an ownership period that is free of problems and inconveniences. We all would like to own a car that doesn't break down, that doesn't depreciate rapidly, that doesn't become uncomfortably expensive or looks used."

OR

"Most customers want to have a great experience; I suspect that you do too. When I say great experience, I mean an ownership period that is carefree and easy. We all would like to own a car that is reliable, that holds value, that is financially responsible and looks great."

Can you *feel* any difference between the two?

Notice that we're not talking about products. It's not of any value to talk about a product because it doesn't solve a problem yet. Also, we don't want to begin talking about problems.

<u>We want to spend some time talking about benefits first.</u> When we only talk about problems people tend to follow Prospect Theory. They develop a cavalier attitude towards risk.

157

Instead, when we talk about benefits people are likely to *feel* warm and fuzzy. They consider what it would be like to adopt the product or service that is going to allow them to continue having that positive feeling. By blending both the benefits and the problems together and doing it in a way that we genuinely seem to be concerned about our customers experience, we are likely to improve our own experience simultaneously.

Another reason we're not talking about the actual product itself yet is because we don't know if it's of any value to the customer yet.

Test it below ⬇

Imagine that you're trying to sell me a lawn mower.

You tell me that this is the greatest lawn mower ever. It mows at different heights, it trims, edges, it has a bag to take care of all the trimmings, it is the best lawn mower in the universe!

Unfortunately, for you, I live on the 18th floor of a condo downtown. Is your lawnmower really a solution for me?

Is your extended warranty really a solution when I think that the Honda that I'm buying is the best car ever?

Is your gap insurance a solution for me when I believe that my insurance with State Farm will take care of everything?

Are your chemicals a solution for me when I think that they're just snake oil?

The list goes on and on, but one thing is clear... if I don't believe that I need it you're not going to sell it to me.

You see, all people are either trying to move away from pain or towards gain. So, if we can engage our customer in a conversation about how they would like this experience to go, they're going to share some pretty interesting things with us...

To begin with if they're talking about prestige, enjoyment, comfort or economy, they're talking about benefits.

However, if they're talking about all the bad things that went wrong with their last car like the lack of economy, mechanical problems, depreciation or anything else like that, they're talking about the discomfort associated with that car, they're moving away from the pain.

By understanding which direction they're going in you can also understand how to most effectively talk with them about providing solutions that work during your presentation.

<u>OBJECTIONS</u>

By now, I think it's fair to say I'm not going to give you some word tracks to overcome customer objections. But in fairness, if I didn't unpack the structure of objections themselves, I think this book would be incomplete.

Aside from a few outliers, there are the 3 main reasons people object to your products and/or presentations:

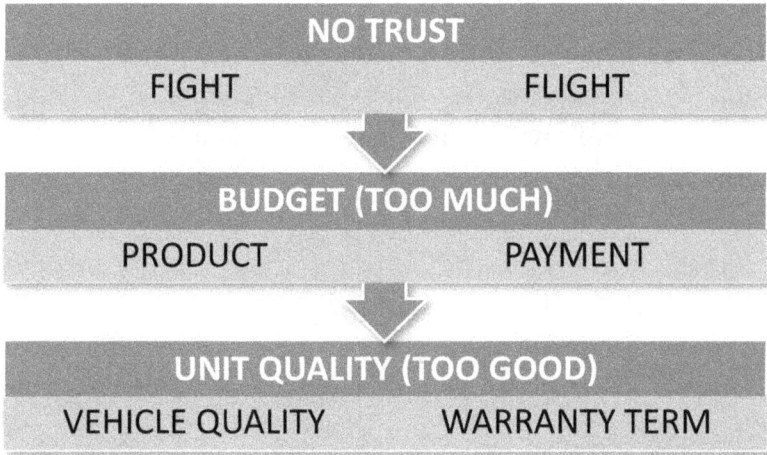

NO TRUST	
FIGHT	FLIGHT

BUDGET (TOO MUCH)	
PRODUCT	PAYMENT

UNIT QUALITY (TOO GOOD)	
VEHICLE QUALITY	WARRANTY TERM

These are the really of the challenges we see. They present themselves in a variety of different ways. Someone that doesn't extend Trust to you might make up a story as a psychological self-defense. Also, known as a lie.

Other concerns, like "budget" and "quality" are in many ways not factual. They are opinions based on beliefs and can be explored and challenged if you demonstrate that you actually care and have some knowledge of what your products do.

Again, a 100% way to close every customer does not exist. You're not going to persuade everyone you meet. But if you can keep your mind from wondering off to your PVR, Penetration or Quota, you'll always be closer to the sale.

Just focus on your customers and their overall experience. Not just the sale, but the ownership experience. If you do that, your profit will occur organically, naturally, and effortlessly.

I sincerely hope you've enjoyed this book and encourage you to reach out with your questions, thoughts and experiences. This material was written specifically for you, with the intent of helping you find more success in the box, but also in life.

Be well,

Lloyd Trushel

Find me at:
www.FandIQ.com

www.ingramcontent.com/pod-product-compliance
Lightning Source LLC
Chambersburg PA
CBHW031533040426
42445CB00010B/521